The TINKERING WOODWORKER

Publisher: Paul McGahren
Editor: Matthew Teague
Design: Paula Chang
Layout: Lindsay Hess & Chad McClung
Photography: Mike Cheung & Paula Chang
Illustration: Mike Cheung
Copy editor: Kerri Grzybicki

Spring House Press
3613 Brush Hill Court
Nashville, TN 37216

ISBN: 978-1-940611-35-8
Library of Congress Control Number: 2015954653
Printed in the United States of America
First Printing: March 2017

The information in this book is presented in good faith; however, no
warranty is given, nor are results guaranteed. Woodworking is inherently
dangerous. Your safety is your responsibility. Neither Spring House Press
nor the author assume any responsibility for any injuries or accidents.

The following list contains names used in *The Tinkering Woodworker*
that may be registered with the United States Copyright Office: AMC;
Apple MacBook Air; Central Machinery; Epstein; *How to Draw Cars the Hot
Wheels Way*; *Mad Men*; *On Printing Types*; Stick Fast; Taschen; *The Big
Book of Creativity Games*; *The Flying Jack . . . I Mean Roger*; Top Care; UL.

To learn more about Spring House Press books, or to find
a retailer near you, email info@springhousepress.com
or visit us at: www.springhousepress.com.

TINKERING MONKEY *presents*

The TINKERING WOODWORKER

WEEKEND PROJECTS FOR HOME, WORK & PLAY

MIKE CHEUNG

SPRING HOUSE PRESS

For Paula, who is always game for silly adventures.

12

62

96

22

68

104

30

Handcrafted by
TINKERING MONKEY

118

38

76

126

48

82

138

CONTENTS

HOME

12   **Entryway Organizer**
A place for everything you'd other wise misplace.

22   **Box-O-Boo**
A clean design to store blades of any style.

30   **Storage Blocks**
Block out some space for all your goodies.

38   **Magnetic Frame**
Is that wood, a magnet, or magic?

48   **The Don Lamp**
Light up your room with class.

WORK

62   **Chip Off the Old Block**
A foolproof device stand is as simple as it gets.

68   **Headphone Hook**
Keep your headphones safe and sound.

76   **Laptop Levitator**
Lift your laptop to keep things chill.

82   **Standing Desk**
Take a stand to give your back a break.

PLAY

96   **Plywood Plinker**
Revel in your rebellious side.

104   **Critter Cavern**
Your fluffy pal deserves only the best.

118   **Beer Tap**
Get a grip on your drinking.

126   **Beer Caddy**
Grab life by the brew.

138   **Bike Rack**
Hang your ride high.

INTRODUCTION

The notion of building something from limited materials, skills, or tools has always intrigued me. Although I've managed to collect a decent workshop full of tools and a head full of knowledge over the past decade, that wasn't always the case. I grew up in the countryside with an insatiable curiosity to know how things worked. Things were taken apart, put back together, and then new things made with the inevitable extra parts left afterward. College rolled around and I studied industrial design, which is really just learning to solve problems and turn those solutions into physical things. Shop skills were forged here, and later honed in the professional design world. I now have my own shop, and run a sign-making business called Tinkering Monkey.

I like to think of myself as a practical woodworker. To me, this means using the tools and skills at hand to create something useful and even beautiful. The projects in this book are more about grabbing some materials and giving things a try, rather than creating show-stopping works of art (no shows were stopped in the making of this book). You should absolutely be proud of what you create, but not precious about each piece you make. Building things with your hands can be frustrating and rewarding within the same moment. The important thing is to learn new things as you build, experiment, and fail. A mistake is really just a practice run. Make enough of them and you'll soon have enough firewood for the winter—or become a master . . . I forget which.

HOME

The time is NOW, or maybe tomorrow, or at least very soon, to kit out your home with handmade projects you can be proud of. Toss those doilies, because here come five projects to make you the envy of the neighborhood.

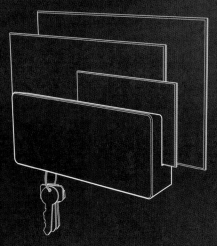

ENTRYWAY ORGANIZER

PAGE 12

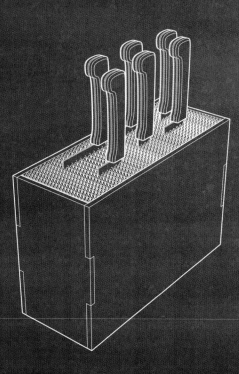

BOX-O-BOO

PAGE 22

STORAGE BLOCKS

PAGE 30

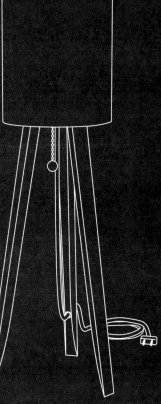

THE DON LAMP

PAGE 48

MAGNETIC FRAME

PAGE 38

ENTRYWAY ORGANIZER

A place for everything you'd otherwise misplace.

"Greetings, your highness!" is what you imagine this humble and faithful servant saying as you enter your home. This quiet guardian of entry manages to hide every bit of hardware, providing subtle assistance as you enter or leave. Strong magnets hidden along the bottom edge are eager to snag your keyring. A gentle tug and they're happy to let go. A slot along the top offers ample room to aid the procrastination of paying up to six bills! It's also perfect for keeping coupons or wads of cash you'd like to remember as you head out the door.

DIFFICULTY

Easy

TOOLS & MATERIALS

- Tablesaw
- Push stick
- Crosscut sled or miter gauge
- Combination square
- Chisel
- Random-orbit sander
- Router table
- ¼" roundover bit
- 45° chamfer bit
- Sanding block
- Drill
- ⅛" drill bit
- ½" drill bit
- Countersink
- Phillips screwdriver
- Polyurethane spray finish

ANATOMY

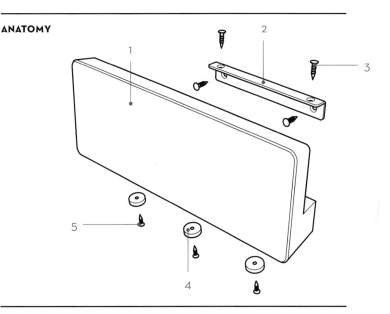

PARTS LIST

No.	Part	Qty	Details
1	Wood block	1	x ½" x 4" x 15"
2	Hanger	1	½" x ½" x 7"
3	Screws for hanger	4	#4 x ½" long
4	Magnets	3	½" diameter
5	Screws for magnets	3	#4 x ¾" long

BEHIND THE DESIGN

Simplicity is the theme for this project. It doesn't get much more simple than a block of wood. The sides are angled to help hide the magnets underneath and the slot on top. The wall mount is easy to install, but completely tucked away.

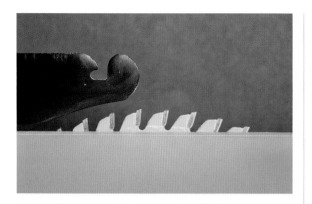

— 1 —

Raise the blade. Set the tablesaw blade height so that at its highest point it rises only about ⅛" above the height of the stock.

— 2 —

Cut it to size. Using a blade guard and push stick for safety, rip the stock to overall width.

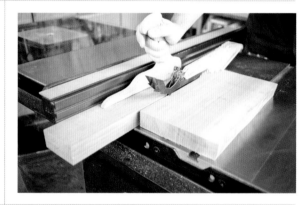

— 3 —

Trim it to length. Using either a crosscut sled or a miter gauge, crosscut the workpiece to rough length, leaving it about ½" longer than final length for now.

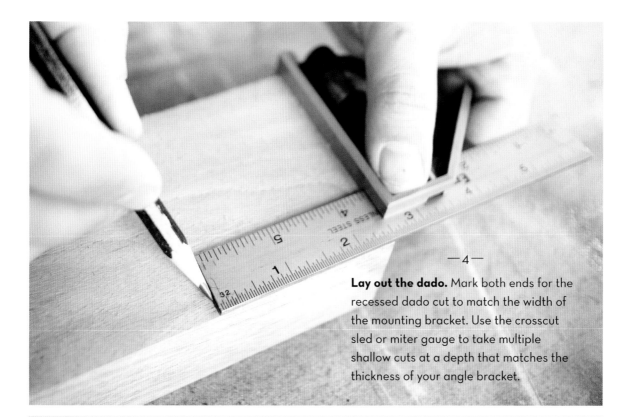

—4—

Lay out the dado. Mark both ends for the recessed dado cut to match the width of the mounting bracket. Use the crosscut sled or miter gauge to take multiple shallow cuts at a depth that matches the thickness of your angle bracket.

—5—

Smooth it out. Use a sharp chisel to clean up saw marks left after cutting multiple passes. Because this surface will be hidden against the wall, it's not necessary to get it super smooth, just flat.

— 6 —

Clean it up. Use a random-orbit sander to create a nice clean face and smooth out the endgrain edges.

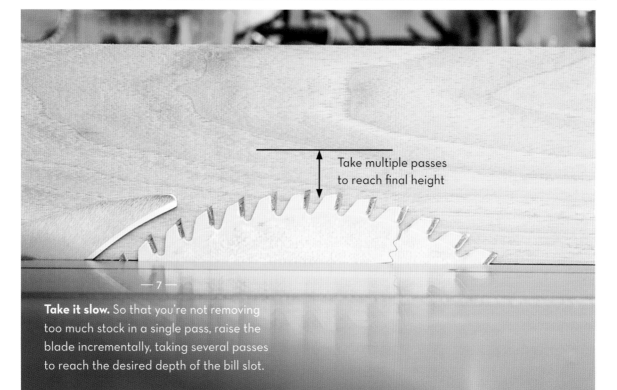

Take multiple passes to reach final height

— 7 —

Take it slow. So that you're not removing too much stock in a single pass, raise the blade incrementally, taking several passes to reach the desired depth of the bill slot.

— 8 —

Create the rabbet. Removing the cutout on the back side of the organizer starts with a rip cut made with the stock held upright against the fence. Take multiple passes, raising the blade between passes until you reach the desired depth of cut.

— 9 —

Set the height. When preparing for the rip cut to remove the waste, use your actual workpiece to set the blade depth.

Remove the cutout. Place the waste side on the outer edge and make a rip cut to free the cutout on the back of the workpiece.

— 11 —

Angle the edge. Adjust the tablesaw blade to a slight angle and make a rip cut on the lower edge of the workpiece.

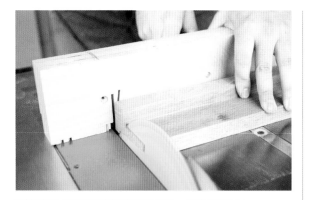

Clean up the cuts. Take it slow when trimming the workpiece to final length so that you get a crisp edge without tearing out the grain at the edges of the stock.

Soften the edges. At the router table, use a roundover bit to knock off the sharp corners.

Sand it smooth. Use spray adhesive to attach sandpaper to the face of a block of wood or plywood. Then use the block to smooth the lower edge of the organizer so that it feels nice and smooth.

—15—

Chamfer the edge. Use a 45° chamfer bit to shape the outside edges of the organizer to knock off the sharp edges.

—16—

Drill for magnets. Drill equally spaced holes on the bottom edge, matching the depth to the thickness of the magnets. Biasing the holes slightly to the front side will help prevent keys from rubbing against the wall.

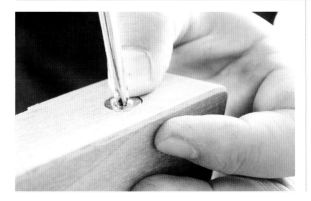

—17—

Add the magnets. Screw the magnets into the holes, sinking them just enough so that their faces sit flush with the lower edge of the organizer.

Add the hanger. The hanger on the lower edge of the organizer fits into the cutout on the back of the organizer. Set the hanger in place and mark out the location of the mounting screws.

—19—

Prepare the bracket. Drill and countersink ⅛" holes in both ends and both sides of the angle bracket.

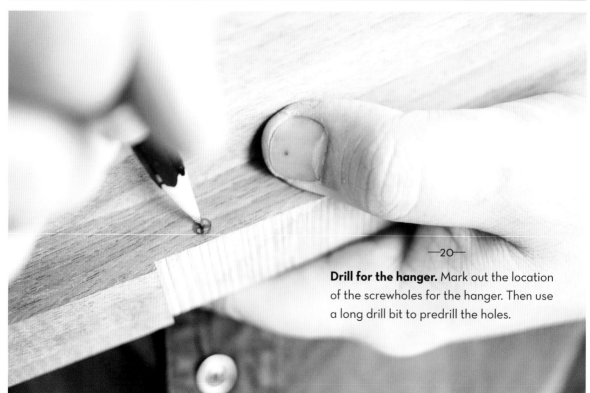

—20—

Drill for the hanger. Mark out the location of the screwholes for the hanger. Then use a long drill bit to predrill the holes.

—21—

Finish it off. A simple spray-can polyurethane makes a quick finish that stands up to a fair amount of abuse.

—22—

Attach the hanger. Begin by mounting the hanger to the wall using screws and, if necessary, drywall anchors.

—23—

Install the organizer. Once the hanger is attached to the wall, set the organizer in place and secure it with a few screws.

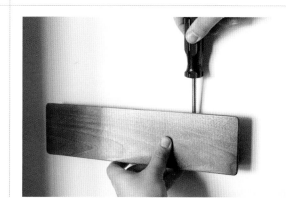

BOX-O-BOO

A clean design to store blades of any style.

Are you still clinging to a few random kitchen knives from back in those dorm days? Perhaps that mini broadsword is still just too sweet to let go. Whatever the case may be, an eclectic knife collection can clash with traditional knife storage. Enter the Box-O-Boo. By housing a veritable forest of bamboo skewers, this kitchen counter cutter keeper is ready to accept any blade from the daintiest paring knife to the heftiest of cleavers.

DIFFICULTY

Easy

TOOLS & MATERIALS

- Tablesaw with dado blade
- Straightedge
- Crosscut sled or miter gauge
- Stop block
- Cyanoacrylate glue
- Wood glue
- Clamps
- Belt sander or sanding block
- Rubber bands
- Bandsaw
- Mineral oil

BEHIND THE DESIGN

The bamboo knife holder is designed to optimize storage of various knife shapes in a compact footprint. Its vertical orientation is meant to fit more comfortably in smaller kitchens or areas with limited counter space.

ANATOMY

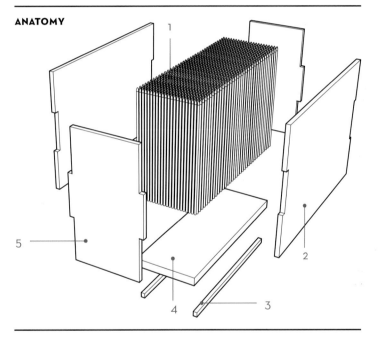

PARTS LIST

No.	Part	Qty	Details
1	Bamboo skewers	pkg.	enough to fill box
2	Walnut sides	2	¼" x 8" x 9"
3	Ledger strips	2	½" x ½" x 8"
4	Bottom	1	¼" x 4" x 8½"
5	Walnut ends	2	¼" x 4½" x 8"

— 1 —

Cut your stock to width. Rip stock to make up all four sides of the box. For the best color and grain match, cut all four sides from a single board.

— 2 —

Mark out the length. Mark and cut the box sides in order—side, end, side, end—so that when you assemble the box, the grain continuously wraps around the corners.

— 3 —

Cut the stock to length. Use a crosscut sled or a miter gauge to cut the box sides. Using a backer board behind the stock helps prevent tearout.

— 4 —

Attach a tall fence. Attach a tall fence to the miter gauge to help secure the stock as you cut the box joints on the ends.

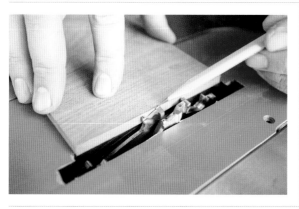

— 5 —

Raise the dado blade. Set the height of the dado set to match the thickness of the stock. (You can achieve the same results with a single blade, but it takes more time and passes to complete the cuts.)

— 6 —

Start your cuts. To establish the void area on the ends, set a stop block to register the stock against the fence as you cut.

— 7 —

Complete the joinery cuts. Incrementally move the stock away from the stop block to remove the remainder of the joinery waste on one end. Then flip the stock and make the same cuts on the opposite end. A block above the workpiece helps keep partially cut stock in the right spot.

— 8 —

Mark the mating joinery. Place the end piece directly on top of the mating side and mark out the location of the finger joint.

— 9 —

Mark the area to remove. To prevent errors, it's a good idea to clearly mark the area to be removed. Note that it is the opposite of the joinery on the ends.

—10—

Move the stop block. Locate the stop block directly off the end. Align the outside of the blade with the edge of the finger joint.

— 11 —

Make the cuts. To establish the beginning and end of the waste area, make cuts with each edge abutting the stop block.

—12—

Mount the ledger strips. Before glue-up, attach small strips of wood along the lower edges of the sides. These ledger strips will be used to locate and secure the bottom of the box.

—13—

Glue it up. Apply beads of glue to the waste areas of each joint then slide the box together.

—14—

Keep it square. Before applying clamps, drop the pre-sized bottom into the box to make sure the assembly stays square during glue-up.

—15—

Clamp it up. Apply clamps spanning the length of the box, making sure the joints close up as you do. Then add a few clamps across the box's length.

—16—

Sand it smooth. A belt sander makes quick work of flushing up the end and sides of the box, but the same could be achieved using a handheld sander or a sanding block.

—17—

Mark up the sticks. Use rubber bands to bundle the bamboo skewers. Then set them in place in the box and mark out their length.

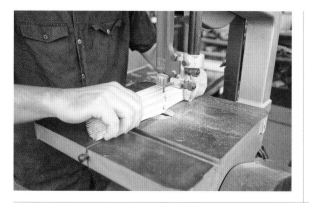

—18—

Trim skewers to length. While they are still held together with rubber bands, batch-cut the skewers to length.

—19—

Lay on a finish. Mineral oil is an inexpensive and food-safe finish that is easy to apply. Simply rub on a few coats using a cotton cloth or paper towel.

—20—

Finish it off. Set the bamboo skewers in place, packing them tightly but so that they can still shift position slightly. Then simply set your knives in place.

STORAGE BLOCKS

Block out some space for all your goodies.

You run a tight ship, but the crew manages to always make a mess. Give those swashbuckling clutter bugs enough storage to tuck everything away with these stackable cubes. Tongue-and-rabbet joints keep things clean and strong enough for the rowdiest pirate to walk the plank on.

DIFFICULTY

Easy

TOOLS & MATERIALS

- Tablesaw
- Measuring stick
- Spacer block
- Miter gauge
- Combination square
- Clamps
- Drill with 2¾" hole saw
- Bandsaw or jigsaw
- Disc sander or sanding block
- Belt sander or sanding block
- Wood glue
- Random-orbit sander
- Clear-coat polyurethane spray

BEHIND THE DESIGN

These stacking cubes nod to all of our favorite interlocking plastic bricks. The through holes that align with the feet also make a great handle to move the cube around. Stack them high or just use one— there's no wrong way.

ANATOMY

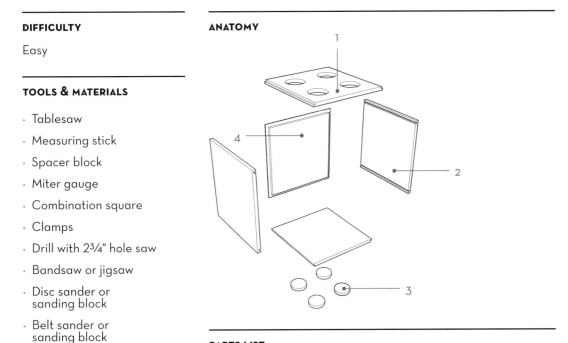

PARTS LIST

No.	Part	Qty	Details
1	Top and bottom	2	½" x 12" x 11½"
2	Sides	2	½" x 12" x 12"
3	Feet	4	2¾" diameter, 3" in from both edges
4	Back	1	½" x 12" x 12"

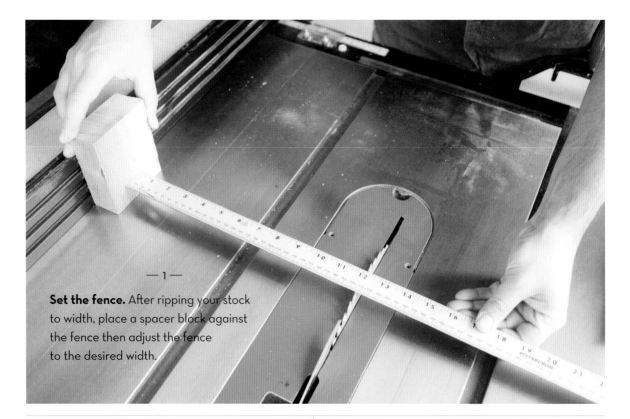

— 1 —

Set the fence. After ripping your stock to width, place a spacer block against the fence then adjust the fence to the desired width.

— 2 —

Position the workpiece. With the stock flush against the miter gauge, position it using the spacer block.

— 3 —

Make the cut. Hold the workpiece firmly in place, remove the spacer block, and make the cut.

— 4 —

Start the rabbet cuts. Once your stock is ripped and crosscut to size, set the blade ¼" from the blade and make a ¼"-deep cut on all of the opposing edges of the side panels.

— 5 —

Finish the rabbet. Set the blade height so the top of the cut is inside the gap left from step 4. This cut creates the rabbet as shown at left.

— 6 —

Create the tongue. Set the blade to the depth and width of the rabbet. Then take two passes with a single blade to cut the ¼" dado and leave the tongue, as shown below.

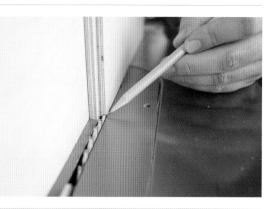

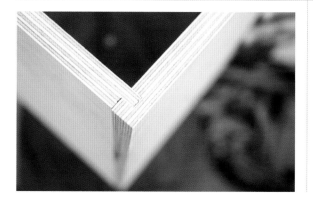

— 7 —

Bring it together. Once the tongue is cut, the corner joints of the box should slide together smoothly.

—8—

Mark hole locations. To find the centerpoint of each hole, set your combination square to 3" and make your marks.

—9—

Cut out the circles. At the drill press, use a hole saw to cut the round openings in the box top.

—10—

Draw the feet. Use a hole drilled with the same hole saw to draw out the shape of the feet on a piece of plywood.

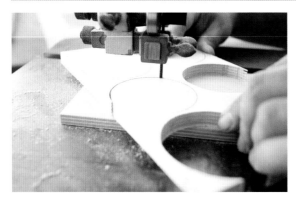

—11—

Cut out the feet. Use a bandsaw or jigsaw to cut the plywood circles that make up the feet.

—12—

Sand them smooth. Use a disc sander or a sanding block to smooth the edges of the circles.

—13—

Clean it up. Remove any pencil marks or fuzz left from sanding the edges by giving the faces a quick pass with a sanding block or over a belt sander.

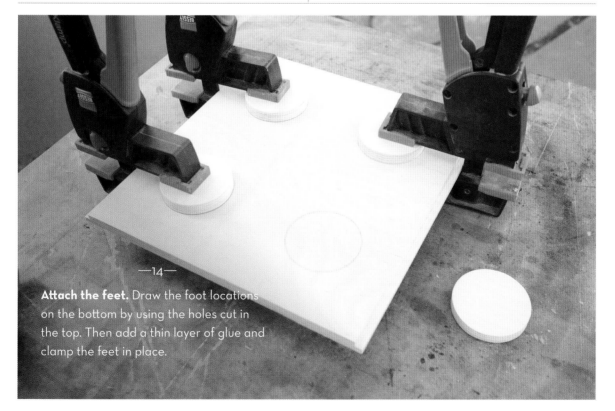

—14—

Attach the feet. Draw the foot locations on the bottom by using the holes cut in the top. Then add a thin layer of glue and clamp the feet in place.

—15—

Lay on the glue. Apply a bead of glue down the grooves and the rabbets cut on the sides and back of the box.

—16—

Bring it together. Set the rabbet into the groove and clean up any mess created by glue squeeze-out.

—17—

Clamp it up. Use a few clamps to close up the joints. The back of the box (not shown) slides into the back and helps ensure that the assembly goes together square.

—18—

Weigh down the back. Instead of adding clamps, use a little weight to make sure the back stays in place during glue-up.

—19—

Clean up the edges. A random-orbit sander does a good job of removing stains from glue squeeze-out and smoothing the corners of the box.

—20—

Apply an easy finish. A simple spray can of clear-coat polyurethane goes on without fuss. Apply two light coats rather than one thick one.

MAGNETIC FRAME

Is that wood, a magnet, or magic?

What if wood were magnetic? For starters, tap dancing would become incredibly entertaining. Hiding a bit of steel just under the surface of some wood creates this mystical magnetic effect. This project is perfect for proudly displaying your favorite '80s hair metal band poster, and then easily swapping it for something a little more tame when the in-laws come by.

DIFFICULTY

Easy

TOOLS & MATERIALS

- Tablesaw
- Push stick
- Miter gauge
- Wood glue
- Pneumatic nail gun or hammer and brads
- Random-orbit sander
- Spray adhesive
- Metal file
- Veneer roller
- Sharp knife
- Sanding block
- Drill and drill bit
- Phillips screwdriver
- Pliers
- Wire snips
- Clear spray lacquer

BEHIND THE DESIGN

Omitting the glass used in a traditional picture frame makes it easy to swap out artwork by moving a magnet.

ANATOMY

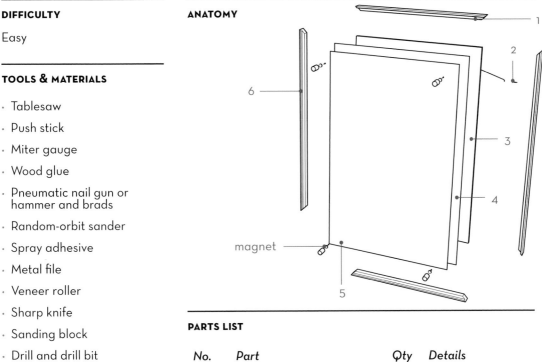

magnet

PARTS LIST

No.	Part	Qty	Details
1	Top and bottom	2	¾" x 1½" x 24"
2	Screw and washer	2	#8, ¾" screws
3	Plywood backer	1	½" x 23½" x 35½"
4	Galvanized metal	1	¹⁄₁₆" x 24" x 36"
5	Peel-and-stick veneer	1	¹⁄₁₆" x 24" x 36"
6	Sides	2	¾" x 1½" x 36"

— 1 —

Reset the blade. Make sure the distance from the fence to the edge of the blade matches the thickness of the plywood. In this case, that is ½".

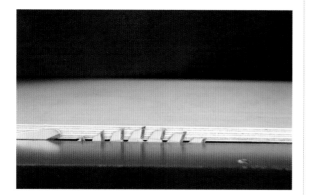

— 2 —

Set the blade height. To ensure that the frame's rabbet is cut to the correct depth, set the height of the blade off the plywood itself. Once complete, the plywood will sit flush to the back of the rabbet.

— 3 —

Make the first cut. Hold the stock on edge to establish the depth of the rabbet. For safety, use a push stick to complete the pass across the blade.

— 4 —

Complete the rabbet. A second cut at the tablesaw removes the rest of the rabbet. Because the depth of the blade matches the thickness of the plywood, the plywood will sit flush in the rabbet.

— 5 —

Determine the length. Remember that your overall length—long point to long point—should match the length of the metal you're using.

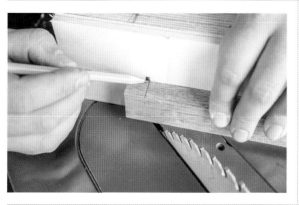

— 6 —

Adjust the miter gauge. Set the miter gauge to 45° and align the mark with the point where the blade enters the miter gauge fence.

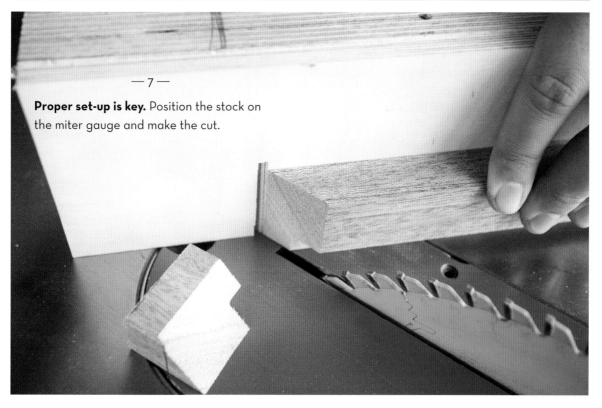

— 7 —

Proper set-up is key. Position the stock on the miter gauge and make the cut.

— 8 —

Set the miter in place. Begin marking the plywood to length by setting the plywood into the rabbet on the stock. Then set the plywood flush to the edge of the rabbet.

— 9 —

Mark out the length. Carefully measure and cut the remaining three rails, using the plywood panel to determine the lengths.

— 10 —

Cut it to size. Set your tablesaw fence to cut the plywood down to size.

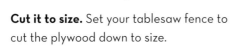

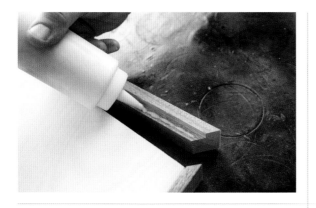

Lay on the glue. Apply glue to the ends of the miters and along the rabbets to help secure the plywood in place on the frame.

—12—

Nail it in place. A few finish nails secure the plywood in place and prevent warping while the glue dries. If you don't have a pneumatic nail gun, a few small brads work just as well.

—13—

Sand it down. Sand down the edges to smooth any trouble spots so the spray adhesive adheres well.

—14—

Apply adhesive to the wood. Lay on an even coat of aerosol spray adhesive to the plywood surface and frame edge.

—15—

Apply adhesive to the metal. To make sure the metal adheres well, you should also apply spray adhesive to the sheet of galvanized metal.

—16—

Bring them together. Make sure the metal is aligned with the plywood and slowly press the metal into place using hand pressure.

—17—

Smooth the edge. If you wind up with the metal hanging over, simply file it flush to the edge.

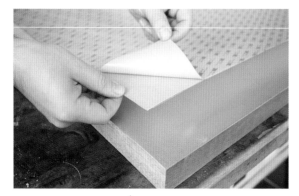

—18—

Remove the backing. Peel-and-stick veneer allows you to skip glue altogether.

—19—

Apply the veneer. After removing the covering, lay the veneer on the metal substrate. Make sure that the veneer overhangs a little on all edges.

—20—

Roll out the bubbles. Use a veneer roller to smooth out any bubbles in the veneer.

—21—

Trim the veneer. Use a sharp knife with a flat face to trim off the excess veneer flush with the wooden frame.

—22—

Smooth it out. Use a sanding block to soften the sharp edge of the veneer.

—23—

Prepare for the hanger. Drill a screw hole about 8" down from the top on both sides of the frame.

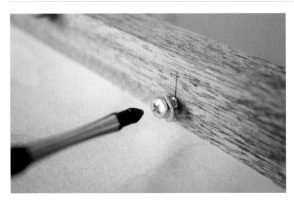

—24—

Drive it home. Install a screw and washer so that at least ½" of thread is buried in the frame but ¼" is still visible.

—25—

Wrap it up. Wrap wire around the screw head twice using a pair of pliers. For a heavy project like this, 14 gauge wire is a good choice. Then trim away any excess using wire snips.

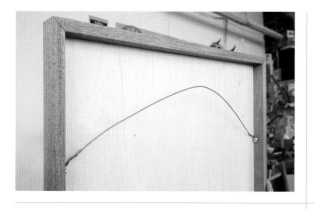

—26—

Hang 'em high. Cut the wire to length so that it has a few inches to spare. Then twist the other end of the wire around the other screw.

—27—

Finish it off. A clear coat of spray lacquer seals and protects the board. Using an after-market spray attachment helps distribute the finish more evenly and makes the process easier.

— QUICK & STYLISH MAGNETS —

A beautiful board can't be adorned with magnets from the pizza joint down the street. Step up your magnet game by installing a rare earth magnet into a hole drilled in the end of a dowel. Some magnets allow you to screw them in place; Others can be epoxied in a hole drilled into the end of a dowel.

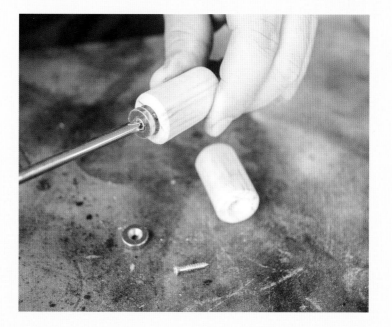

THE DON LAMP

Light up your room with class.

The Don Lamp sprang to life after binge-watching AMC's hit show, Mad Men. While not up for starting a Manhattan ad agency, I was completely game to decorate our house with the swanky stylings seen on the show. After a fruitless search for a tripod lamp with legs connecting under the shade, I decided to just make one myself.

DIFFICULTY

Moderate

BEHIND THE DESIGN

The Don Lamp lives up to its namesake with its striking good looks and 1950s sensibility. The simple, elegant lines of this tripod lamp complement a variety of home decors. The cord is kept tidy and out of the way with a simple pass-through in one of the legs. This functional and beautiful detail prevents the lamp from tipping should the cord get snagged.

TOOLS & MATERIALS

- Tablesaw
- Tablesaw sled, miter gauge, or miter saw
- Taper cutting jig
- Router table
- ⅛" roundover bit
- 22° beveled router bit
- Belt sander
- Sanding block
- Socket wrench
- Handheld drill with ⅜", ³⁄₁₆", and ⅛" drill bits
- Countersink bit
- Bandsaw
- Drill press with ⁷⁄₁₆" bit
- Belt sander or sanding block
- Cyanoacrylate glue
- Screwdriver
- Clear finish of choice

ANATOMY

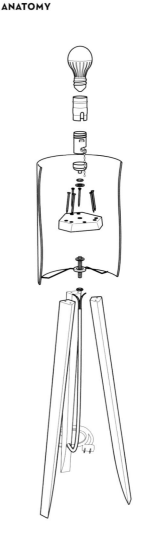

PARTS LIST

No.	Description	Qty	Details
1	Bulb socket	1	Pull chain
2	Brass nut	2	⅛-IP
3	Brass washer	2	⅜"
4	Wood screws	6	#8, 2" long
5	Lamp shade	1	10 to 12" drum
6	Steel nipple	1	⅛-IP x 2"
7	Lamp cord	1	8'
8	Legs	3	1" x 1½" x 21"
9	Wall plug	1	Two wire
10	Lamp harp *optional*	1	
1	Threaded spacers *optional*		
12	Pull chain knob *optional*	1	

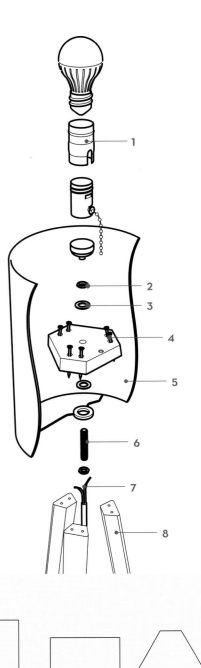

— **VARIATION ON THE LAMP** —

In our experience with making these lamps, we found it sometimes difficult to obtain that perfectly shaped and sized lamp shade. Adjusting the design of the lamp to match the shape of the shade might be necessary. We found that generally matching the width of the lamp's stance with the bottom edge of the shade worked well, to a point. It's always a good idea to try a couple of sketches before starting to cut wood.

— 1 —

Cut three leg blanks. Using 1"-thick hardwood lumber (also called 4/4), cut the three leg blocks approximately 1½" wide and 21" long. You may need to alter the length depending on the type of shade you would like to use. Bonus points if you use scrap wood.

— 2 —

Cut a 10° bevel. Cut a bevel on one end of each leg blank using a tablesaw sled, miter gauge, or miter saw. The bevel determines which face is outward, so this is an opportunity to slant the bevel downward toward the more interesting grain pattern.

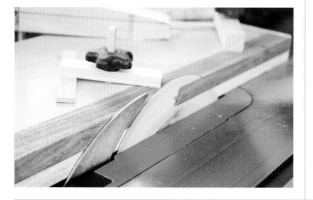

— 3 —

Shave off ¼" from each side. Set up a taper jig to start cutting from the edge at the start. The jig will need to be adjusted to cut the second side, so perform the initial cut on all three legs before switching sides. Or not, if you just like spending extra time in your workshop.

— 4 —

Check the taper. A subtle change in width will look more elegant than very steep angles. Think "carrot" more than "traffic cone."

— 5 —

Round the edges of one face. Place the leg with the 10° bevel facing down. Use a ⅛" roundover bit to round just the sides and narrow end. Do not round off the 10° beveled wide end.

— 6 —

Prepare a 22° bevel bit. This bit has a half-inch shank, making it more robust when removing bigger swaths of wood. Keep the carbide clean of pitch and resin for the smoothest cuts.

— 7 —

Adjust the router. Flip the leg so the 10° bevel is facing up. Adjust the 22° beveled router bit height so the bearing engages just below the roundover.

— 8 —

Bevel the sides. Again, cut only the sides and narrow tip, avoiding the 10° cut wide end. Use a steady pace that is slow enough to reduce tear-out, but fast enough to prevent burning. A second pass usually helps to smooth things out.

— 9 —

Curve the tip. A belt sander makes quick work of blending the inside corner of the tip. A parabolic curve that gradually fades into the flat inside surface works well visually.

—10—

Check the curve. Carefully blending the curve around the end of the leg will make it look nicely finished. This image shows the before on the left and the after on the right.

— 11 —

Hand sand the sides. Smooth the sides with a sanding block wrapped with 220- to 400-grit sandpaper. This will remove any remaining tool marks or irregular bumps left after routing. It also looks really cool to anyone watching you work.

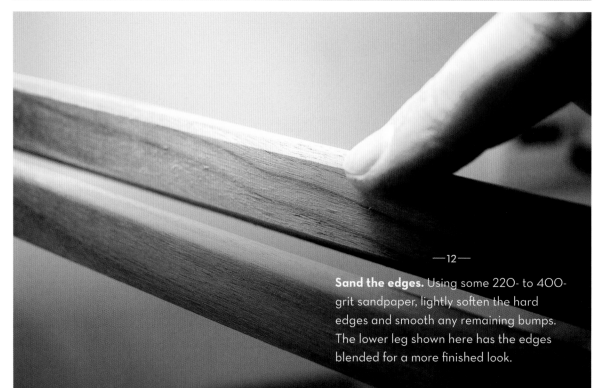

— 12 —

Sand the edges. Using some 220- to 400-grit sandpaper, lightly soften the hard edges and smooth any remaining bumps. The lower leg shown here has the edges blended for a more finished look.

— 13 —

Drill the cord-passage hole. Use a drill bit that is just a little larger than the diameter of the lamp cord you plan on using. Drill the hole in the center of one leg, about 2" from the bottom end. Pick the leg with the most interesting inside grain pattern.

—14—

Countersink the hole. Adding a shallow countersink to the front and back of the cord-passage hole will give it a more finished look.

—15—

Cut the tripod topper. Use a bandsaw to cut a six-sided puck from the same wood the legs are made of. It should be roughly 3" wide, with the three alternate sides the same width as the tops of the tripod legs.

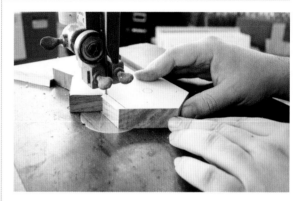

—16—

Drill the center. Use a 7/16" drill bit to drill a hole in the center of the topper. The bit should be just a bit wider than the threaded steel nipple that will be used to assemble the lamp.

—17—

Sand the sides of the topper. Adding a 10° bevel to the sides can tidy up the look of the topper, but isn't necessary if it will be hidden by a lampshade. Sand the flat sides of the topper and knock off any sharp edges with a piece of sandpaper or a belt sander.

—18—

Temporarily attach the legs. A little CA (cyanoacrylate) glue will be enough to quickly bond the legs to the topper. Wood glue and clamping can be used, if you have extra time and like doing it the hard way.

—19—

Drill pilot holes. Use an ⅛" drill bit to drill pairs of holes through the topper and into the top of each leg. Keep the bit in-line with the legs to prevent the bit from coming out of the side. Countersink the holes after drilling.

—20—

Screw the pieces together. Enlarging the pilot hole in just the topper will help prevent the screws from forcing the two pieces of wood apart.

—21—

Lightly assemble the socket. Thread in the steel nipple to the bottom of the bulb socket. Be careful to prevent the halves of the socket from snapping together. Place the assembly in the tripod topper.

—22—

Mark the pull-chain hole. Hold the pull chain loosely to determine where it naturally falls and mark the spot with a pen. Running the chain through the topper keeps it from tangling if the chain is let go under tension.

—23—

Drill the pull-chain hole. Use a drill bit large enough to allow the chain to freely move through the hole. A light countersink helps to guide the chain beads through the hole.

—24—

Finish the tripod. Finish the tripod with your preferred clear coating. A few coats of wipe-on polyurethane brings out the beauty in the wood, while leaving the lamp well protected. Use some bear grease instead if you plan on putting the lamp in a log cabin.

—25—

Tie UL knots. Tying a knot like this helps prevent the connections from pulling loose should the cord get yanked. If your parts allow, tie one at both the socket and plug ends.

—26—

Assemble the lighting components. The order in which parts are put together may vary depending on the shape and orientation of lampshade used. It can be very helpful to lay parts out on a table to reduce the chance of error.

—27—

Personalize the chain pull. An optional finishing touch is a custom chain pull. Snip the chain a bit below where it exits the bottom of the tripod topper and use a coupler to attach the new pull at your desired length.

WORK

Who says work has to be boring? This suite of work-friendly projects will have you buzzing along like the busy bee that you are. Impress your coworkers or just your cat with these useful projects that actually make cubicle life worth living.

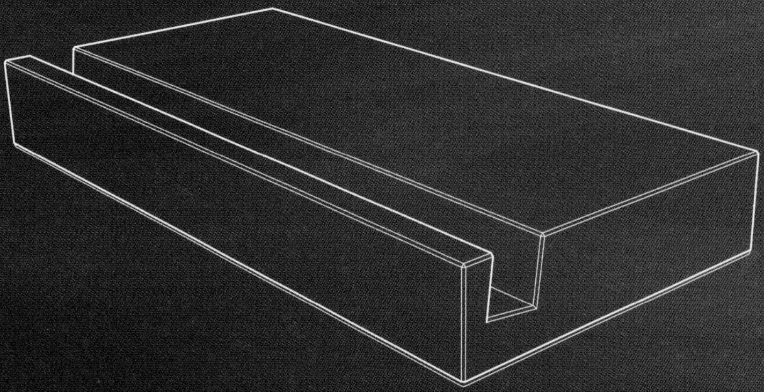

CHIP OFF THE OLD BLOCK

PAGE 62

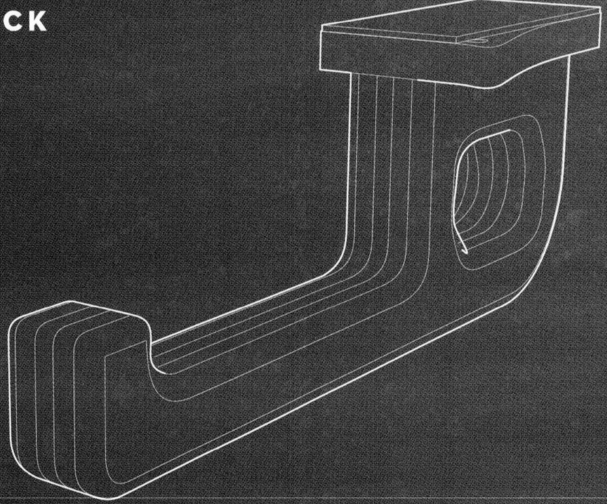

HEADPHONE HOOK

PAGE 68

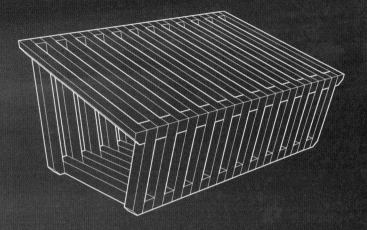

LAPTOP LEVITATOR

PAGE 77

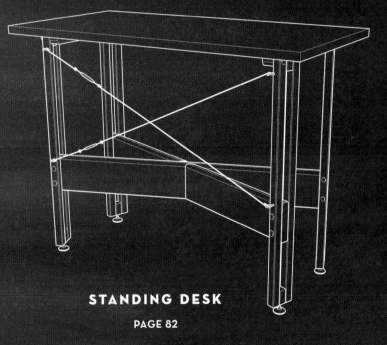

STANDING DESK

PAGE 82

CHIP OFF THE OLD BLOCK

A foolproof device stand that's as simple as it gets.

Have the urge to watch cat videos for hours on end? This sleek, minimal wooden device stand is sturdy enough so you can hit replay to your heart's desire, and portable enough to slip into your bag for long plane flights. No gimmicks, no fuss, no fancy setup. Just a slotted stand to give you the perfect viewing angle, so you can quickly tune in—wherever you want.

DIFFICULTY

Easy

TOOLS & MATERIALS

- Tablesaw
- Push stick
- Random-orbit sander
- Dado blade
- Featherboards or push sticks
- 220-grit sandpaper
- Measuring tape
- Sharp knife
- Straightedge
- Wood finish of choice

BEHIND THE DESIGN

The saying "Necessity is the mother of invention" rings true for this project. A desire to view a tablet at a comfortable angle while typing, and a lack of excess time, led to the creation of this simple project. All you need is just about any scrap piece of wood and a little time.

ANATOMY

PARTS LIST

No.	Description	Qty	Details
1	Lumber	1	1" thick
2	Cork contact paper	1	Sized to fit

— 1 —

Select a piece of wood. It should be flat and about 1" thick. Wood that is free from knots and warping will be much easier to work with. Rip the wood to width with the tablesaw. Raise the blade until the valleys between the teeth are at the top of your board.

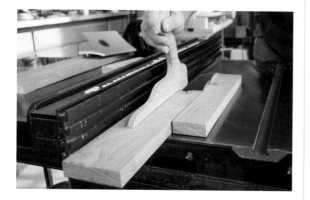

— 2 —

Rip it to width. Pass the wood completely past the blade with a push stick. Press lightly toward the fence side to keep the wood aligned. Cut slightly wider than needed, then trim the other side off at the correct dimension for a clean cut.

— 3 —

Smooth it out. Sand the board with a palm sander. Random-orbit sanders leave a nice finish. Depending on the quality of wood, you may have to start with heavier grit (smaller number) sandpaper and work your way up to about 220.

— 4 —

Install the dado blade. Tilt it and adjust the height. For 7 to 10" tablets, a stack of $\frac{7}{16}$" at 7° tilt and about $\frac{5}{8}$" height works well. If the intended device is very thick or heavy, adjust the cut accordingly.

— DIFFERENT TYPES OF DADO BLADES —

There are a few ways to achieve a wide slot on a tablesaw. Stacked dado blades will produce the cleanest cut, followed by a wobble blade, and finally multiple cuts using a standard blade. Each method has its advantages and disadvantages.

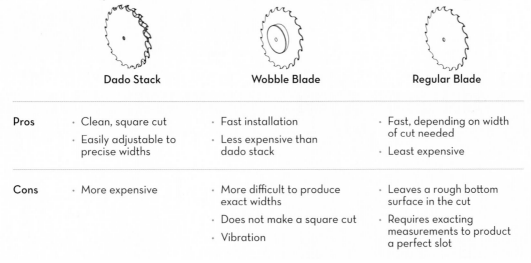

	Dado Stack	Wobble Blade	Regular Blade
Pros	· Clean, square cut · Easily adjustable to precise widths	· Fast installation · Less expensive than dado stack	· Fast, depending on width of cut needed · Least expensive
Cons	· More expensive	· More difficult to produce exact widths · Does not make a square cut · Vibration	· Leaves a rough bottom surface in the cut · Requires exacting measurements to product a perfect slot

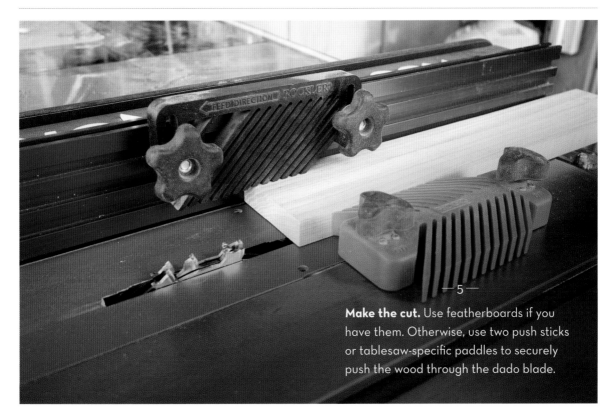

Make the cut. Use featherboards if you have them. Otherwise, use two push sticks or tablesaw-specific paddles to securely push the wood through the dado blade.

— 6 —

Inspect the cut. A dado stack removes much more material than a standard saw blade. This means the wood will be met with more resistance and needs a firm grip and slower speed when passing by the blades. If you notice an aberration, cut the slot once more.

— 7 —

Knock it off. Use sandpaper to break the sharp edges. Lightly sanding the edges with 220-grit sandpaper will make the wood more finger friendly. The sooner the edges are softened, the less likely a splinter will happen.

— 8 —

Measure and mark the wood. Base your measurements on the device you'd like to use with the stand. For tablets, the width in portrait orientation works well.

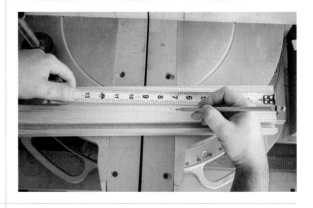

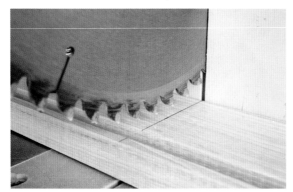

— 9 —

Cut it to width. Align the cut to the outside of the saw blade. Cut carefully to avoid too much tear-out around the slot. The tablesaw or even a handsaw can be used for this step.

—10—

Sand the ends after cutting. There may be some tear-out of the wood fibers. Sand along the edges and try not to pull any large fibers out of place.

—11—

Trace the block. Allow a little extra space from the edge of the wood. If graphite gets on the wood, just lightly sand it off. Cut the cork with a sharp knife and straightedge. Make sure fingers are out of the way. Several light cuts are safer than a single heavy cut.

—12—

Attach the cork. Peel the backing and carefully place the block on the sticky side. Press the cork on with firm pressure for a good bond. Carefully trim the excess cork. Move the knife carefully, using the wood as a guide. A low angle works better to reduce tearing off bits of cork.

—13—

Finish the job. Inspect for bits of adhesive or cork protruding from the edges. Sand any remaining sharp edges or errant cork bits that might remain. Apply your preferred wood finish. A clean cloth and wipe-on polyurethane or spray polyurethane works great for this project.

HEADPHONE HOOK

Keep your headphones safe and sound.

Even the best of us need to take a break from rocking out. For those times, rely on this smart, unobtrusive hook to quickly stash your headphones away until it's time to crank the volume back up. It works great mounted under a desk or shelf.

DIFFICULTY

Easy

TOOLS & MATERIALS

- Tablesaw with zero-clearance insert
- Combination square
- Push stick and featherboard
- Belt sander or sanding block
- Wood glue and brush
- Clamps
- Templates (see tinkeringwoodworker.com)
- Spray adhesive
- Drill press with ¾" Forstner bit
- Bandsaw
- Spindle sander
- Belt sander
- Router table
- ⅛" roundover bit
- 220-grit sandpaper
- Wood finish of choice

BEHIND THE DESIGN

The headphone hook is inspired by high-end kitchen knives. The core provides strength, while the outer scales flesh out the body.

ANATOMY

PARTS LIST

No.	Description	Qty	Details
1	Heavy-duty double-sided tape	1	
2	Top plate	1	1¼" wide x 2¼" long
3	Outer hook layers	2	¼" x 2" x 6"
4	Inner hook layer	1	⅛" x 2" x 6"

— 1 —

Prepare to cut the boards. You will use the tablesaw to cut ⅛"-thick planks from the 2 x 12" boards. Thin lumber is not always easy to find. Set the blade height to just over half the height of your board.

— 2 —

Make the first cut. Set the fence to produce ⅛" cuts for the inside layer. Be sure to use a push stick and, if possible, a featherboard.

— 3 —

Make the second cut. Flip the board and cut the other half. A zero-clearance tablesaw insert is recommended. The tight tolerance to the blade prevents the cut pieces from falling into the saw.

— 4 —

Examine the cut. The cut should be nearly perfect if your saw is well maintained. If the cuts are misaligned, use a belt sander or sanding block to smooth the surface. Cut two strips at ¼" (outside layers) and one strip at ⅛" thick (inside layer), using contrasting wood.

— 5 —

Apply the glue. Spread a thin layer of wood glue on one face of one outside strip and the inside strip. Cover the entire area for best results.

— 6 —

Stack the pieces. Place the glued surfaces together. Repeat the gluing procedure with the top outside strip. Try not to get glue on the outer faces of the wood to reduce cleanup after it dries.

— 7 —

Clamp the stack. Spread out the pressure evenly, and keep an eye on alignment. Wood glue will act as a lubricant, making it easy for the layers to slide if clamped a little askew. Allow 2 to 12 hours to dry, depending on environment.

— 8 —

Check the glue-up. The layers should be tight and flat after gluing. It is not necessary to remove glue drips, unless they interfere with the wood lying flat.

— 9 —

Attach the template. Draw your template or download one at tinkeringwoodworker.com and attach it to the layers using a light dusting of spray glue. If you decide not to design your hook on a computer, sketching on the wood with a pencil works fine. Just be sure to leave about 2" of flat area at the top of the hook to attach the top plate.

—10—

Drill out the holes. To make cord organization holes, use a ¾" Forstner bit. It is helpful to mark the center points for an elongated hole. Keeping both holes horizontally aligned reduces the amount of sanding needed afterward.

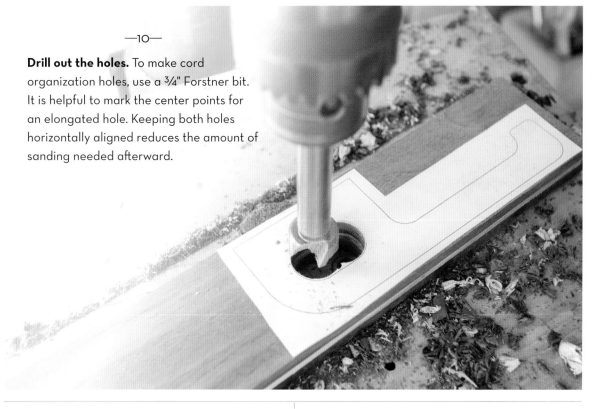

—11—

Bandsaw the hook. Cutting as close to the lines as possible can greatly reduce the amount of time needed for sanding. Slow and steady yields the best results on a bandsaw. This is also a good time to cut the top plate out—it should be wider and longer than the hook's surface.

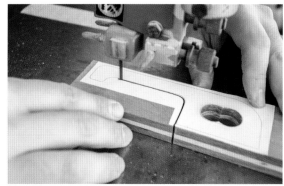

—12—

Sand the interior curves and surfaces. A spindle sander works best, but a drum sander in a drill press works as a great alternative. Take plenty of time to get the surfaces nice and true.

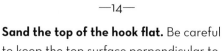

—13—

Sand the exterior curves and surfaces.
Use a firm grip and gentle pressure on the belt sander to sand irregularities from the edges. Use a continuously moving, rolling technique on the curved sections.

—14—

Sand the top of the hook flat. Be careful to keep the top surface perpendicular to the sides. A disc sander would also work great for this step. Also sand the edges of the top plate.

—15—

Prepare the router table. Use an ⅛" roundover router bit. Carefully set the height of the bit so the bottom of the rounded curve is tangent to the surface of the table.

—16—

Round the edges. Round both sides and the cord hole of the hook. Use extra caution when working with a router table. Always move against the blade's spinning direction to reduce the chances of the bit throwing the wood.

—17—

Prepare for finishing. Clean up any router marks with 220-grit sandpaper. Sand in the grain direction to avoid scratches. Glue the top plate in place. You can drill a screw hole in the front corner for very heavy headphones.

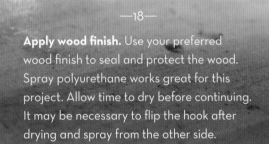

—18—

Apply wood finish. Use your preferred wood finish to seal and protect the wood. Spray polyurethane works great for this project. Allow time to dry before continuing. It may be necessary to flip the hook after drying and spray from the other side.

—19—

Mount the hook. Cut and apply a strip of heavy-duty double-sided tape to the top plate. Use firm pressure to attach the tape before mounting the hook under a desk or shelf. Try holding headphones up before sticking the tape on to visualize where to place the hook.

LAPTOP LEVITATOR

Lift your laptop to keep things chill.

Are you cursed with a massive laptop and a minuscule desk? Are you constantly flooding your workspace with spilled coffee? If so, a laptop stand is just what the doctor ordered. By elevating your precious computer, space is freed up for storage, while bringing the screen up to an ergonomic viewing height.

DIFFICULTY

Easy

TOOLS & MATERIALS

- Templates (see tinkeringwoodworker.com)
- Tablesaw
- Push stick
- Stop block
- Clamps
- Wood glue
- Disc sander or sanding block
- Belt sander or sanding block

BEHIND THE DESIGN

Stacks of variable length rods repeat to create this simple stand. By making the structure from a repeating pattern, the design is easily scalable to a variety of device sizes. Simply lengthen a dimension or add another stack for larger computers.

ANATOMY

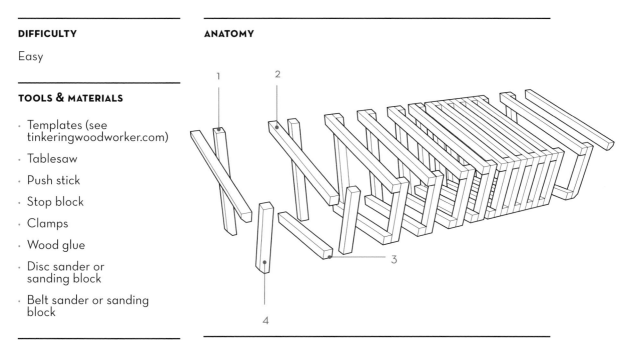

PARTS LIST

No.	Part	Qty	Details
1	Back pieces	12	½" x ½" x 5¾"
2	Top pieces	13	½" x ½" x 8"
3	Bottom pieces	11	½" x ½" x 6"
4	Front pieces	12	½" x ½" x 3⅞"

— 1 —

Rip the strips. At the tablesaw, rip all of the stock for the stand to the same width and thickness. I chose a width of ½". For safety, be sure to use a push stick to finish the cut.

— 2 —

Set the length. Use a crosscut sled or miter gauge to cut the stock for the back pieces to length. Begin by positioning a stop block to the desired length.

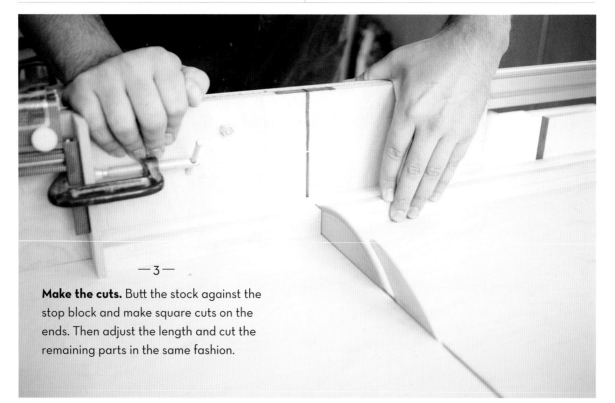

— 3 —

Make the cuts. Butt the stock against the stop block and make square cuts on the ends. Then adjust the length and cut the remaining parts in the same fashion.

—4—

Use the drawings. Seeing the finished shape on a template makes it easy to keep parts organized as you work.

—5—

Glue it up. Add a drop of glue to each joint and glue up sets of four pieces.

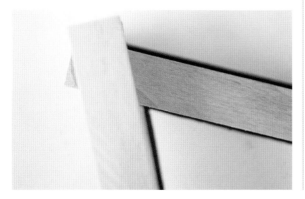

—6—

Ignore the angles. Instead of making angled cuts on the ends of each piece, assemble the parts with square cuts. You will sand away the excess after glue-up.

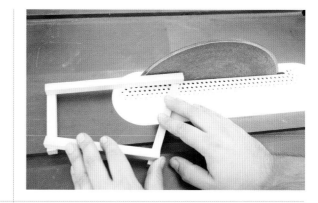

— 7 —

Sand away the waste. A disc sander or a sanding block removes the angles on the ends quickly.

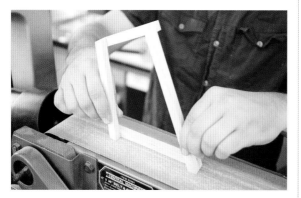

— 8 —

Smooth the sides. With the waste removed from the joints, smooth each outside face using a belt sander or a large sanding block.

— 9 —

Stack 'em up. Assemble the stand by adding a drop of glue at each intersection and stacking them up. Once stacked up, a little weight on the top keeps everything tight while the glue sets.

—10—

Add extras. Once the stand is together, add an extra length of stock to both ends of the top.

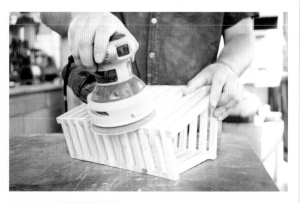

—11—

Clean it up. A quick sanding removes any glue squeeze-out and levels any spots that may be slightly proud.

—12—

Soften the edges. When you pick up the stand, you don't want to feel sharp edges. At the tablesaw, make a quick angled cut on the two ends of the top.

STANDING DESK

Take a stand to give your back a break.

Do your back a favor and build a standing desk. Scientists have studied the backsides of many people to determine that standing for part of the day keeps you healthy as a horse. Working while standing feels great, and might actually add some years to your life. Who doesn't want more years at the end to yell at the kids on the lawn?

DIFFICULTY

Advanced

TOOLS & MATERIALS

- Tablesaw with miter gauge
- Wood glue
- Clamps
- Thickness planer
- Templates (see tinkeringwoodworker.com)
- Vise
- Drill with 1/8" and 3/8" bits
- Phillips screwdriver
- Small scrap of rubber (optional)
- Socket wrenches
- Combination square
- Tape measure
- Hand saw
- Chisel and mallet
- Hammer
- Flush cut saw or backsaw
- Sanding block or block plane
- Wood finish of choice

PARTS LIST

No.	Description	Qty	Details
1	Solid-core door	1	1⅜" x 30" x 60"
2	Trim strips for desktop edges	3	¼" x 1⅜" x 60"
3	Lag bolts and washers	8	½" x 3"
4	Screw eyes	4	#6, 1¼" long
5	Redwood lumber legs	8	1⅜" x 1⅜" x 42"
6	Leg spacers	8	1⅜" x 1⅜" x 6"
7	Casters or feet and matching T-nuts	4	⅜" thread
8	Steel rods (2 of each size)	4	⅛" x 40" & ⅛" x 10"
9	Turnbuckles	2	3"
10	Lag bolts and washers	8	⅜" x 6"
11	Screws	14	2½"
12	Ledger strips	2	1½" x 3½" x 24"
13	Douglas fir stretchers	2	1½" x 6" x 4'
	Finishing nails	8	1"

ANATOMY

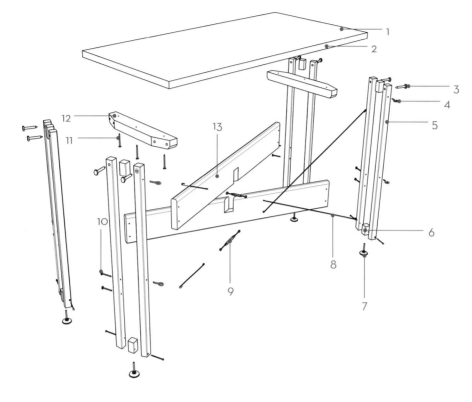

BEHIND THE DESIGN

The standard size built here uses 42"-long legs, but when building for a particular person—yourself or someone else—determine the leg length based on the user's elbow height. The top of the desk should be at or slightly below the elbow when standing.

The strong table legs and architectural cross beams keep the desk sturdy and grounded. The cross beams also act as a footrest for tall chairs, which makes the desk function well for both sitting and standing.

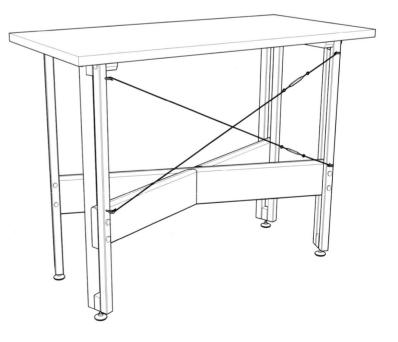

— 1 —

Prepare the legs. Cut the leg stock and leg spacers to length. Then pair them up to create the legs; two full length legs and two short spacers for each assembly.

— 2 —

Keep it neat. Use a sanding block or a block plane to cut 45° chamfers on the ends of each workpiece.

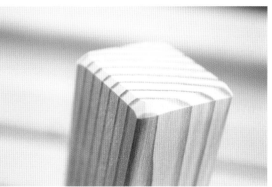

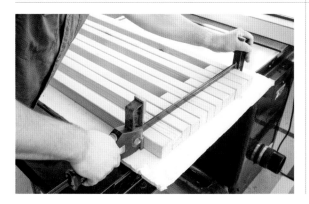

— 3 —

Build the legs. Add a thick layer of glue on mating surfaces and use clamps to pull the legs together. You can assemble all four legs in one glue-up; just remember not to apply glue between each of the legs.

— 4 —

Prepare the X-beams. The X-beams lend the structural support to keep everything sturdy and square. For a clean look, begin by giving them a pass through the planer.

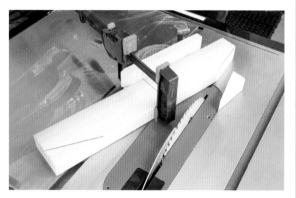

— 5 —

Shape the ends. The legs attach to the ledger strips on tapered ends that match the width of the legs. To cut the tapers, use your miter gauge set to a sharp angle and be sure the workpiece is clamped in place. For cutting templates of desks of various sizes, go to tinkeringwoodworker.com.

— 6 —

Small details make the difference. Angle the ends of the legs at the chop saw or tablesaw to lend a more refined look.

— 7 —

Screws add strength. I used to make these desks to sell, so I would shoot in the screws before the glue was dry as additional structural support and to clamp the glue. This step could be omitted, because glue alone is likely good enough.

— 8 —

Drill for casters. With the bottoms of the
legs held upright in a vise, drill holes to
accept the threaded caster sleeves.

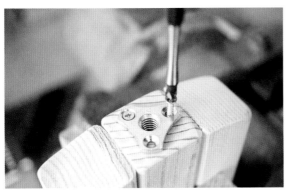

— 9 —

Add the sleeve. A few screws secure the
housing for the casters into the bottoms of
the desk legs.

— FEET OR CASTERS? —

Whether you choose permanent feet or casters is largely
determined by your planned use for the desk. If it will live in one
spot, feet are more secure. For a mobile unit that makes its way around the
office, casters are the way to go. Installation is largely the same.

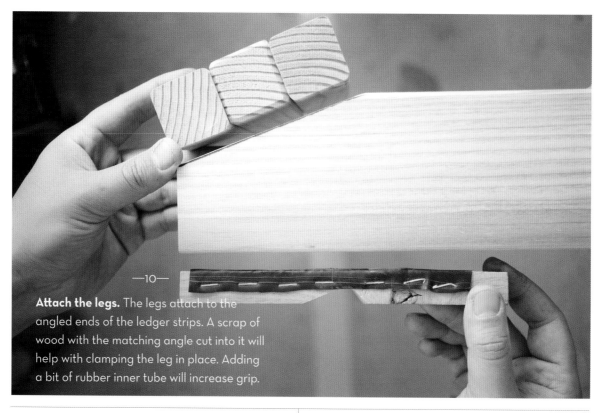

—10—

Attach the legs. The legs attach to the
angled ends of the ledger strips. A scrap of
wood with the matching angle cut into it will
help with clamping the leg in place. Adding
a bit of rubber inner tube will increase grip.

—11—

Cover all the bases. Make sure the legs
attach square to the ledger strips. Start
with the leg clamped upright in a vise.
Then clamp the ledger strip in place using
a square to check the angle. Sink a few
bolts to secure everything in place.

—12—

Prepare for the top. Drill a few pilot holes
into the ledger strips. These will be used to
secure the desktop to the ledger strips.

—13—

Mark stretcher locations. The X-beams slide into voids between the assembled legs. Mark their location on the legs roughly 28 to 30" down from where the top surface of the desk will be. This places the X-beams a natural "floor" distance from the top when seated.

—14—

Attach the stretchers. Slide one stretcher in place and add clamps to hold it. Then drill pilot holes and drive a few lag screws into place.

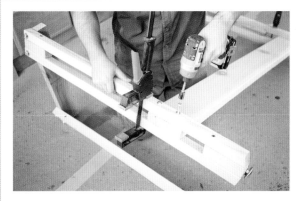

—15—

Bring the stretchers together. With one stretcher attached, set the other in place on top of it. Then mark out the location on the edges of each stretcher.

—16—

Saw it out. Mark out the depth of the stretcher location to half the depth of the stretcher. Then saw down to the lines on each of the stretchers.

—17—

Remove the waste. On each of the two stretchers, use a chisel and mallet to knock out the waste between your two saw cuts.

—18—

Bring it together. With one stretcher secured in place and the other positioned in the voids between the legs, slide the two workpieces together. If necessary, adjust the fit with a chisel. Then bolt the stretcher in place.

—19—

Fine-tune the base. Steel rods attached with turnbuckles are used to reinforce the base and keep everything square. Drive eyehooks into the legs to accept the turnbuckles.

—20—

Reinforce the base. Attach the turnbuckles and steel rods to the base. Screw them tightly into place, but make sure they aren't so tight that they distort the shape of the frame.

—21—

Edge the desktop. Almost any strong, flat surface can be used for the top. Shown here is a solid-core door that has been cut shorter on the tablesaw. Some hardwood trim cleans up the cut end for a nicer look.

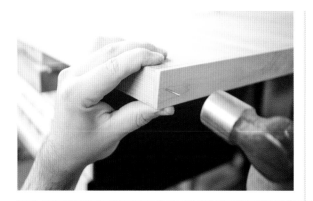

—22—

Secure it in place. Glue and a few nails are all it takes to attach the hardwood trim.

—23—

Trim the trimwork. Use a flush cut saw or backsaw to cut the ends of the trim so that all of the joints are flush. Then smooth it out with a sanding block.

—24—

Attach the top. A few lag screws driven through the ledger strips secure the top to the base. Apply your finish of choice or leave the raw wood, as you wish.

— STANDING DESK ADD-ON —

A folding add-on to your existing sitting desk is a quick way to achieve the benefits of a standing desk without committing to the full-size standing desk. This is an example of something that can be built in an afternoon using only ¾" plywood, a few screws, and hinges. The legs angle outward at 18° for stability, and fold flat for easy storage.

PLAY

Go play outside! This utterance is going the way of the dodo as video games take over. Reclaim that call of the wild, the reckless yearning of wind in your hair, and the risk of a broken bone. If you build these playful projects, I guarantee you'll be at one with the natural world.

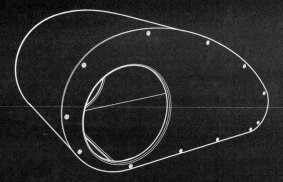

PLYWOOD PLINKER

PAGE 96

CRITTER CAVERN

PAGE 104

BEER TAP

PAGE 118

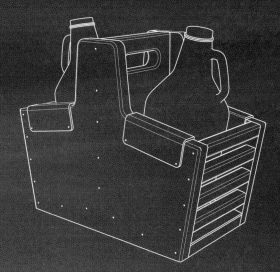

BEER CADDY

PAGE 126

BIKE RACK

PAGE 138

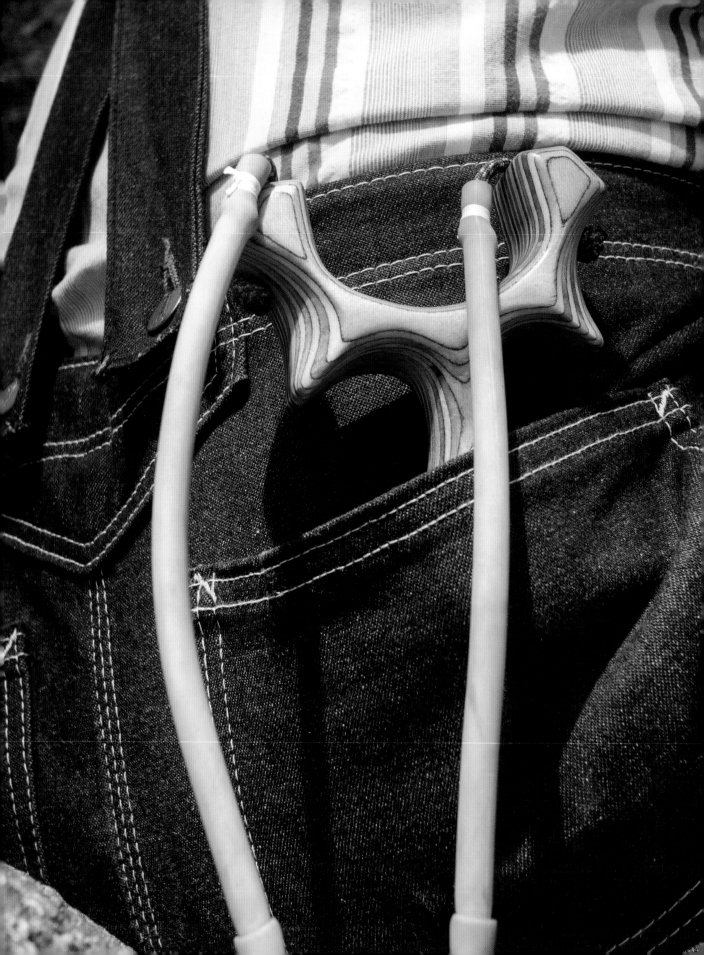

PLYWOOD PLINKER

Revel in your rebellious side.

Dennis the Menace may have been a slingshot OG, but his simple tree branch lacked the modern features of this ultra custom, ultra precise plinker. Shaping the subtle plywood curves into a perfect fit will be one of the great joys of your life. (Careful, though; target practice or ping pong balls only.)

DIFFICULTY

Easy

TOOLS & MATERIALS

· Wood glue and brush
· Clamps
· Template (see tinkeringwoodworker.com)
· Spray adhesive
· Bandsaw
· Spindle sander
· Router table
· ¼" roundover bit
· File or rasp
· Sandpaper
· Hand drill
· Countersink bit
· Clear spray lacquer
· Lighter
· Needle-nose pliers

BEHIND THE DESIGN

Plywood's cross-directional construction makes it perfect to shape into organic forms while maintaining strength. The topographical lines revealed while crafting the wood act as both a symmetry guide and decoration.

ANATOMY

PARTS LIST

No.	Description	Qty	Details
1	Slingshot pad	1	⅛" x ¾" x 1¾"
2	Rubber tubing	2	1¼" diameter x 8"
3	Dental floss	1	as needed
4	550 paracord	2	4" long
5	Handle	3	¾" plywood
6	Eye hook	1	½" long
7	Paracord loop	1	3" long

— 1 —

Prepare the blank. Start by face-gluing two thicknesses of ¾" plywood together, making sure they are sized to accomodate the template.

— 2 —

Glue it up. Apply plenty of clamps to lend even pressure and prevent voids when you cut the blank to shape.

— 3 —

Apply the template. The easiest way to get the pattern to the blank is to simply print out the pattern (from tinkeringwoodworker.com) and glue it to the blank using a shot of spray adhesive.

— 4 —

Cut it to shape. Use a small bandsaw blade (¼" or less) to cut out the shape of the slingshot.

— 5 —

Sand it smooth. Using a spindle sander quickly cleans up the inside edges. No spindle sander? You can achieve the same thing using sandpaper wrapped around a dowel.

— 6 —

Aim for symmetry. When sanding, check the profile frequently and aim for a pleasing, symmetrical shape.

— 7 —

Soften the edges. Use a ¼" roundover bit chucked into your router table to round all edges of the slingshot.

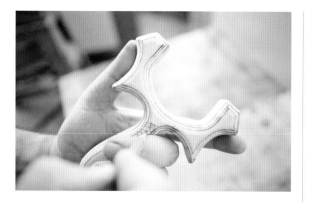

— 8 —

Make it comfortable. Test the fit of the slingshot in your hand, mark out the area where your index finger falls, and then file it away.

— 9 —

Fine-tune the shape. Use a rasp or file to remove the sharp edges that would otherwise rub against your hand.

—10—

Finishing touches. On a small piece with lots of shapes and roundovers, a quick smoothing with handheld sandpaper is easier than trying to use a power sander.

—11—

Choose your bit. The diameter of the bit should match the diameter of the cord used on the slingshot.

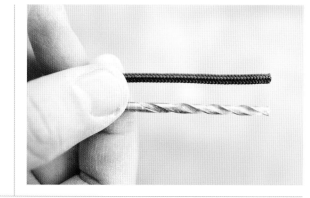

—12—

Drill it out. Aim for a hole that will allow you to tie off the cord in an out-of-the-way location, and take care to replicate the hole position and angle on both sides.

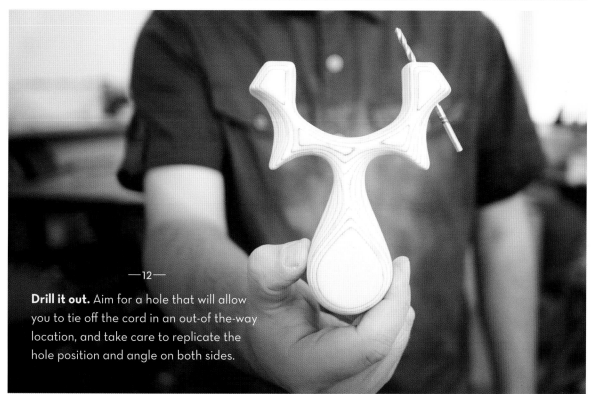

—13—

Make way for knots. Use a countersink chucked into your hand drill to remove stock at the top of the slingshot so that your rope can move easily.

—14—

Apply a finish. A spray lacquer provides a beautiful and protective finish. To ease the finishing process, suspend your slingshot using a rope strung through the hole in the end.

—15—

String it up. Install cord through both holes on the slingshot and tie knots on all four ends.

—16—

Light it up. To prevent the cord from unraveling, use a small torch or a lighter to singe the ends of the rope.

—17—

Make it match. For balanced shooting, make sure the length of cord on the two sides is the same.

—18—

Install the tubing. Use needle-nosed pliers to secure the end of the rope, then stretch the tubing over the pliers.

—19—

Tie it off. Use dental floss to secure the end of the tubing below the knot on the cord. Wrap the dental floss numerous times around the tubing and tie it off.

—20—

Add a handle. To secure the slingshot around your wrist, add an eyehook and length of cord to the bottom of the slingshot.

CRITTER CAVERN

Your fluffy pal deserves only the best.

A pet is one of the family, and often higher in the pecking order than some of the people. Give them the not-so-humble abode they deserve with a Streamliner-inspired house straight out of a 1950s vision of the future. Little Fluffy will probably get a big head and gloat among the neighborhood pets, but that's okay, 'cause who's a perfect little fuzzywuzzy?

DIFFICULTY

Moderate

TOOLS & MATERIALS

- Tablesaw
- Template (see tinkeringwoodworker.com)
- Spray adhesive
- Drill with ½", ⅟₁₆", and countersink drill bits
- Jigsaw
- Bandsaw
- Spindle or drum sander
- Disc or belt sander
- Router table with flush-trim bit and ⅜" roundover bit
- Tape measure
- Hammer and nail
- Wood glue
- Clamps
- Screwdriver
- String
- Tin snips
- Work gloves
- Cylinder, such as packing tube
- Pneumatic staple gun or hammer and brads
- Food-safe finish of choice

PARTS LIST

No.	Description	Qty	Details
1	Wood rods for crossbeams	8	¾" x ¾" x 14"
2	½" plywood board for sides	2	12" x 22"
3	Wood screws	24	#8, ¾" long
4	½" plywood board for base	1	15¾" x 12¹³/₃₂"
5	Carpet	1	15" x 12
6	Aluminum sheet	1	14" x 41"

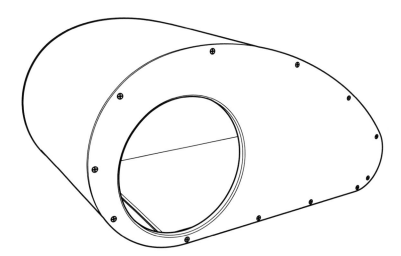

ANATOMY

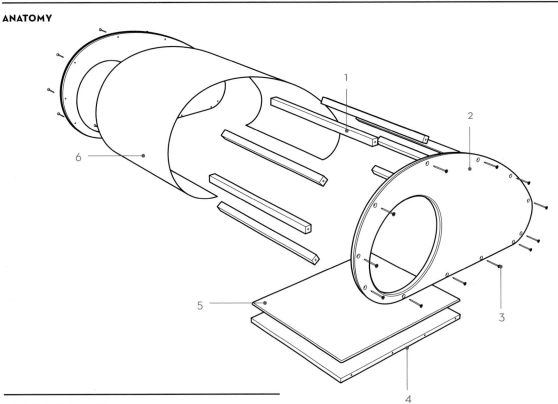

BEHIND THE DESIGN

Custom teardrop camper trailers are the inspiration for this project. Their simple construction of side walls and a single piece of roofing material scales perfectly to pet size.

— DESIGN VARIATIONS —

For the pet house in our shop we mimicked the lines of a teardrop trailer, but feel free to form the shape however you'd like.

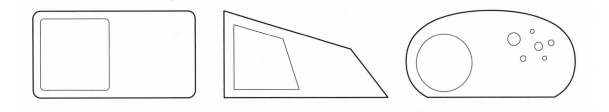

— 1 —

Cut the sides. Use a tablesaw or circular saw to cut the side walls to rough size. The base will be cut later, determined by the final size generated from the sides.

— 2 —

Sketch or trace the design. Either sketch a design directly onto the wood of one side, or print out the templates available at tinkeringwoodworker.com and attach them with a dusting of spray adhesive.

— 3 —

Drill and cut the doorway. Drill a hole near the inside edge of the doorway. Use a jigsaw from this hole to cut the doorway out completely.

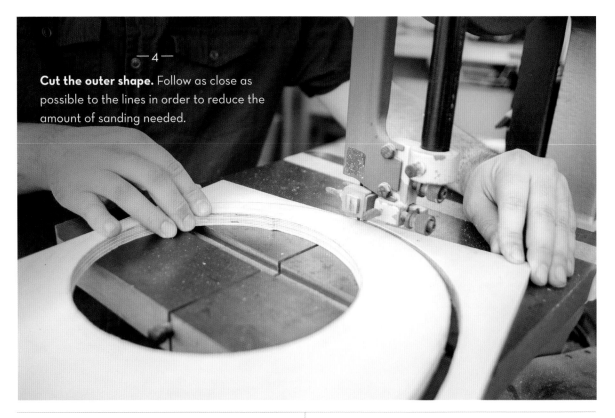

— 4 —

Cut the outer shape. Follow as close as possible to the lines in order to reduce the amount of sanding needed.

— 5 —

Sand the doorway. One benefit of a circular doorway is being able to easily sand the full circumference on a spindle or drum sander.

— 6 —

Sand the exterior. Use a disc or belt sander to smooth the bandsaw cut marks along the exterior shape of the side wall. Smooth transitions will look best and keep the aluminum roof from bending.

Trace the second sidewall. Use the now-smoothed first sidewall to trace the pattern on the second side. A sharp pencil will ensure that the transfer is as close to the same size as possible. Repeat the cutting and sanding steps to duplicate the first side.

— 8 —

Adjust the router bit. Set up the router table with a flush-trim bit, but with a smaller bearing installed. Allow ⅛" of untrimmed material to remain above the blade edge.

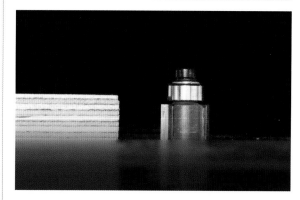

— 9 —

Cut the rabbet. Cut along all sides except the base. Multiple passes will ensure that there are no bumps remaining. The cut surface will be hidden by the aluminum roof, so don't worry about light burn marks appearing.

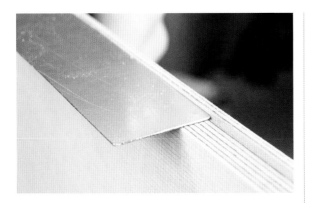

—10—

Check the depth. This step-down will provide protection from the sharp edges of the aluminum once it's installed. Now is a good opportunity to sand all the edges smooth.

—11—

Round over the doorway. Use a ³⁄₈" roundover bit to soften the edge of the doorway.

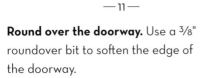

—12—

Cut the cross members. Rip some ³⁄₄" x ³⁄₄" square rods on the tablesaw and trim them to 14" long. Mark the centers of each end and drill ¹⁄₁₆" pilot holes.

—13—

Trace the cross members. Align the edge of a cross member along the rabbet cut and trace around it. Once again, a freshly sharpened pencil is your best friend. This needs to be done on the inside surface of only one wall.

—14—

Repeat the tracing. Keep tracing the tip along the edge of the rabbet cut approximately 3 to 4" apart. Span the entire top side of the wall, beginning and ending at the ends of the flat base.

—15—

Mark the centers. Use a small ruler to mark the centers of each traced square by drawing an X using the four corners.

—16—

Drill and countersink. Drill 1/16" pilot holes through all the traced squares. Countersink the holes along the outside surface. Consistent depth on the countersinks looks super-professional.

—17—

Stack and transfer the locations. Carefully align the two side walls and tap a nail through the holes to transfer their locations to the second sidewall. Repeat the drilling and countersinks, paying close attention to the outside/inside orientations.

—18—

Cut the base. Match the width of the base to the length of the cross members.

—19—

Prepare the base. The base should span the length of the bottom of the house, and provide enough flat surface for comfortable entry. After cutting to size, trace a line along the top edge while it is lined up along the bottom. Drill and countersink pilot holes, transferring them to the second sidewall as well.

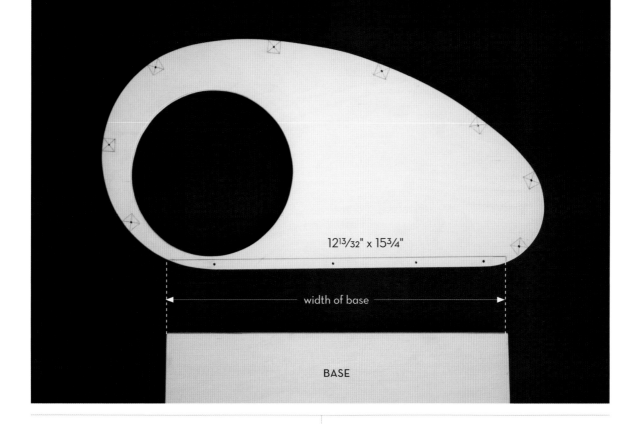

12¹³⁄₃₂" x 15¾"

width of base

BASE

—20—

Clamp and drill. Carefully align the sidewalls and base and clamp into place. Feel free to use a little wood glue at this point, although the screws should be enough to hold everything together. Deepen the base pilot holes after clamping.

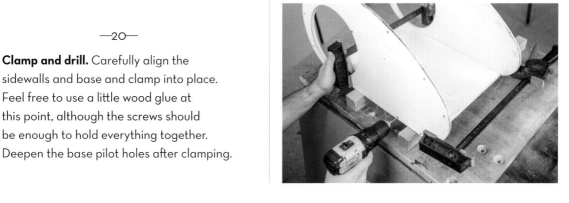

—21—

Install screws. Using a drill or screwdriver, install the small screws along both sides of the base. Be careful not to over-tighten and strip the wood fibers inside the holes.

—22—

Partially install the screws. Install the screws along the top side of the walls so the tip is just barely protruding from the inside.

—23—

Snap in the cross members. Using the screw nubs, snap in the cross members. It's helpful to give the screws a couple more turns after snapping into place, so that installing the adjacent cross member doesn't dislodge all that hard work. Tighten everything up nice and straight.

—24—

Measure the top length. Run a piece of string along the rabbet cut from the very front to the very back. This will determine how long to cut the aluminum top.

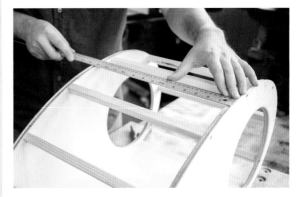

—25—

Measure the top width. Carefully measure the distance between the rabbet cuts. Subtracting about 1/32" will ensure that the aluminum will fit easily into the space.

—26—

Mark and cut the aluminum. Carefully measure and mark the aluminum sheet. Trim it to size with the tin snips, being careful of the sharp edges. Smooth cuts while maintaining contact against the blades reduces the number of "splinters" that need to be filed off afterward.

—27—

Curve the aluminum. Pre-curving the aluminum around a cylinder such as a packing tube or rolling pin makes installation much easier. Wear gloves during this step to reduce the risk of nicks and cuts.

—28—

Match the curves. Keep gently curving the aluminum until it almost rests on the house on its own. Have patience—it may take a few tries to get it just right.

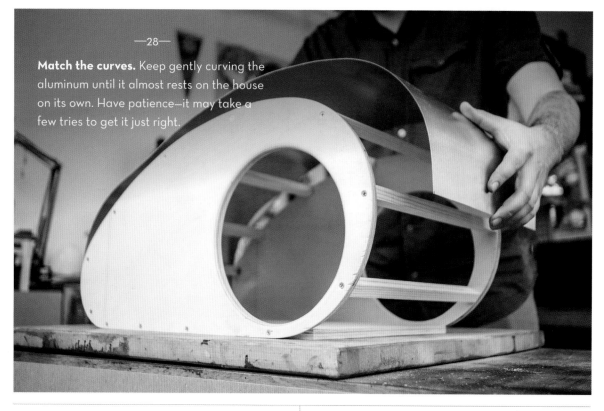

—29—

Secure the edges. Use a pneumatic staple gun or brads and a hammer to attach the edges of the roof to the side walls. Start at the middle and work your way toward the two ends, making sure there are no lumps or swells.

—30—

Finish the wood. This particular house is intended for a rabbit, which means there's a chance for a bit of nibbling. A natural wax or oil finish should keep your little pal safe. Use unscented finishes to avoid irritating sensitive little noses.

—31—

Add the bling. Wall-to-wall carpeting adds some comfort and sound dampening. Cutting a small notch in the corner will make it easy to remove the carpet for cleaning.

BEER TAP

Get a grip on your drinking.

You've spent days learning the science, hours in preparation, and weeks waiting for fermentation. Finally! The day has come to taste your concoction. Sure, a twist of a knob will get the job done, but why not top off all that hard work with a custom tap handle that screams, "I am brewmaster, eat my suds!"

DIFFICULTY

Easy

TOOLS & MATERIALS

- Tablesaw
- Push stick
- Wood glue and brush
- Clamps
- Straightedge
- Bandsaw
- Belt sander
- Lathe
- Gouge, 1" or similar
- 120- and 220-grit sandpaper
- Sanding block or random-orbit sander
- Vise
- Drill with bit sized to ferrule
- Wrench
- Beeswax
- Spray polyurethane finish

BEHIND THE DESIGN

The honest-to-goodness inspiration for this project was a pair of bowling shoes. A stripe up the middle and good times to be had when in use— what could be more perfect?

ANATOMY

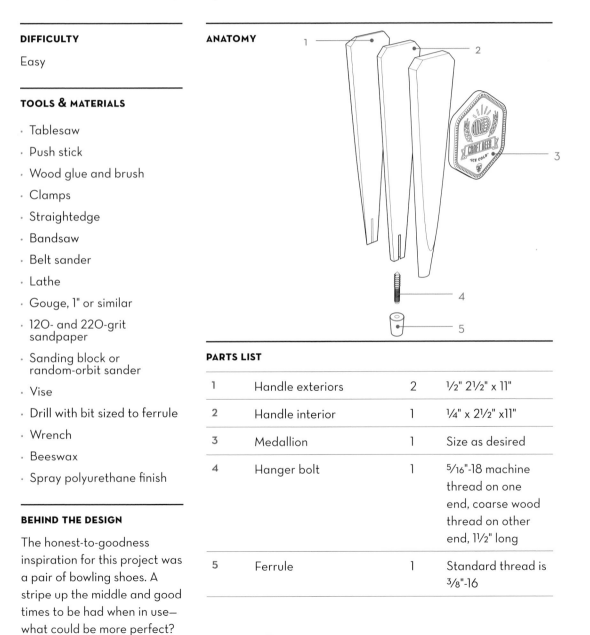

PARTS LIST

1	Handle exteriors	2	½" 2½" x 11"
2	Handle interior	1	¼" x 2½" x11"
3	Medallion	1	Size as desired
4	Hanger bolt	1	5/16"-18 machine thread on one end, coarse wood thread on other end, 1½" long
5	Ferrule	1	Standard thread is 3/8"-16

— 1 —

Prepare the stock. Rip all three layers of stock to the same width at the tablesaw.

— 2 —

Lay on the glue. Use a roller or brush to apply an even coat of glue to both sides of the mating faces.

— 3 —

Clamps are your friends. Work from the middle out, applying pressure evenly across the full length of the assembly.

— 4 —

Start at the base. Find the center of the ends by drawing diagonal lines from corner to corner. Then center the ferrule on the end and trace the diameter.

— 5 —

Draw out the shape. Mark pencil lines that taper from the diameter of the ferrule to the top edge of the stock.

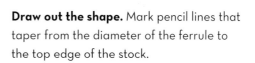

— 6 —

Bandsaw just outside the lines. Removing the bulk of the stock prior to turning will make later work at the lathe much quicker.

— 7 —

Clean it up. Use a belt sander to sand down to your layout lines, smoothing the bandsawn edges of the stock as you work.

— 8 —

Start turning. Mount the lathe centers on the centers of the two ends of the stock. Begin turning by hogging off the lower end so the tap is round at the bottom. Use a 1" gouge, or whatever you have on hand.

— 9 —

Take stock of the shape. As you turn, work from the bottom to the top. Aim for a shape that progresses from round at the bottom to square at the top.

—10—

Sand it smooth. Begin sanding with 120-grit sandpaper while the tap is still in the lathe. Then finish off with 220 grit.

—11—

Check the faces. If the flat sections need any cleanup, you can do so with a sanding block or random-orbit sander.

—12—

Drill out the tap. Following the specs for the particular ferrule you plan to use, drill into the centerpoint on the bottom of the tap. Be sure to keep the bit aligned as you drill.

—13—

Get ready to tap the tap. Aluminum ferrules are inexpensive. You can sacrifice one to help thread the hole before installing the chrome ferrule. If not, simply screw two nuts onto each other on the threading rod.

—14—

Prepare for the ferrule. Use a wrench to drive the threading rod into the bottom of the tap handle.

—15—

Install the ferrule. When installing the actual ferrule by hand, it helps to lubricate the threads with a little beeswax.

—16—

Refine the shape. Using the belt sander, knock off the hard corners by shaping chamfers on the ends.

—17—

Lay on the finish. A simple spray can of polyurethane lends protection and just enough shine.

—18—

Establish a brand. You can throw on a sticker, carve, or paint the tap itself. Or, as shown here, order a small laser-etched medallion of your own design.

BEER CADDY

Grab life by the brew.

Two parts grog and one part weather-beaten treasure chest come together to create this party animal. Add some bedazzling with brass studs and a bit of battle charring and you've found all you need to create the coolest caddy in the cove. This double growler caddy makes it easy to bring your favorite brew with a generous handle fit for a hand, hook, or peg.

DIFFICULTY

Moderate

TOOLS & MATERIALS

- Tablesaw
- Thickness planer
- Template (see tinkeringwoodworker.com)
- Spray adhesive
- Drill with 1" Forstner bit and ⅛" bit
- Coping saw or jigsaw
- Spindle or drum sander
- Punch
- Bandsaw
- Sanding block
- Router table with ¼" roundover bit
- 120- to 220-grit sandpaper
- Tablesaw sled or chop saw
- Wood glue
- Hammer and nail
- Straightedge
- Clamps
- Cyanoacrylate glue
- Propane torch
- Flathead screwdriver

ANATOMY

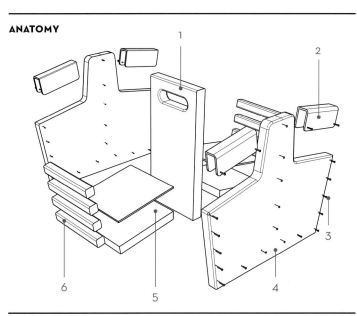

PARTS LIST

No.	Description	Qty	Details
1	Handle board	1	¾" x 5⅝" x 11½"
2	Felt or leather	4	⅛" x 3½" x 4"
3	Small brass screws	40+	#4 , ½" long
4	Sides	2	¾" x 12" x 15"
5	Base boards	2	¾" x 5⅝" x 5²⁹⁄₃₂"
6	Side rails	8	¾" x ¾" x 5⅝"

BEHIND THE DESIGN

Flame torching wood has been a finishing method for centuries. The powerful look is enhanced with brass trimmings, and the growlers are tipped outward to embrace the party time look.

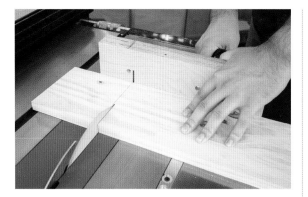

— 1 —

Cut the three interior main parts. Rip-cut a length of the pine board to a width ¼" wider than the growlers intended for this project. Crosscut the two base boards and central rib/handle board.

— 2 —

Plane down the sides. Plane the stock for the sides to approximately ½" thickness. Planing the sides creates a more refined look, but this can be skipped if you don't have a planer.

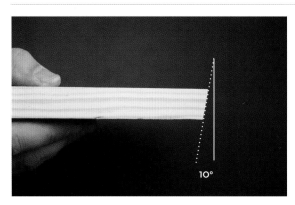

— 3 —

Cut a 10° bevel. Cut a bevel on the inside edge of each base board. This will butt up against the central handle board.

— 4 —

Cut the handle. Using a 1" Forstner bit, drill out the two ends of the handle, approximatel 4" wide. Remove the wood between the two holes with a coping saw or jigsaw.

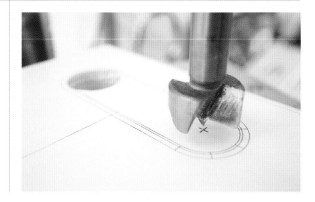

— 5 —

Sand the handle. Spindle sand the handle to smooth the edges. If you don't have a spindle sander, a drill-mounted drum sander or a hand file can be used.

— 6 —

Trace and punch one side. Trace the template available at tinkeringwoodworker.com. Mark the screw holes using a punch.

— 7 —

Saw the side. Carefully follow the template to cut out the sides. A thinner bandsaw blade will make cutting the curves easier, but requires more concentration to maintain a smooth edge on the straight parts.

— 8 —

Clean up the bandsaw marks. Use a sanding block to smooth the flat edges, and a spindle or drum sander for the inside curves.

— 9 —

Trace the first side. Tracing the first side ensures a symmetrical project, in case there are slight variations from the template.

—10—

Round over the edges. Use a ¼" roundover bit to round the outside edges of the two side parts and the handle area. Leave the base of the sides square. Smooth everything with sandpaper afterward.

— 11 —

Smooth it out. Use a piece of 220-grit sandpaper to smooth any leftover blemishes after routing the handle area.

— 12 —

Set up for crosscuts. Set up a tablesaw sled or chop saw to cut the rods down. Use the central handle board to set up a stopper so the slats are exactly the same length as the other interior parts.

— 13 —

Crosscut slats. Once the saw is set up, cut eight side rail pieces to length.

—14—

Mark felt. Mark and cut felt for the tops of the two base boards. Leather works too, but may discolor from condensation over time.

—15—

Glue felt. Use a little wood glue to attach the felt or leather to the tops of the base boards. A little weight, say, from a full growler can keep things flat.

—16—

Drill pilot holes. Drill out the pilot holes previously marked with a punch. The holes will help align the interior parts.

—17—

Transfer holes. Use a nail to transfer the drilled holes to the second side. A light tap with a hammer should be enough.

—18—

Strike a line through the holes. Use a straightedge to draw a line through the holes.

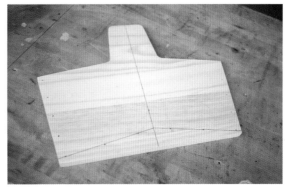

—19—

Mark the interior board locations. Align the interior boards to the lines, and lightly trace their outer edges. Start with the central handle board.

—20—

The two base boards should nestle up against the central handle board and slope downward to the bottom corner of the side.

—21—

Glue and clamp the interior boards. Following the guidelines, carefully glue and clamp the interior boards to just one side. Gluing both sides at once can lead to misalignment.

—22—

Glue on the second side. After the glue has dried at least an hour, remove the clamps and glue on the second side.

—23—

Clamp vertically. It's a good idea to flip the caddy upright for the final clamping, to ensure the two sides are parallel along the bottom.

—24—

Place the slats. A drop of cyanoacrylate glue can be used to secure the slats temporarily. Use a section of extra slat to space them evenly.

—25—

Deepen the pilot holes. Drill into the interior boards and slats to deepen the pilot holes in preparation for the brass screws. If you prefer standard screws, you may want to countersink the holes so the heads are flush with the exterior surface.

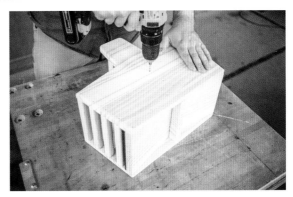

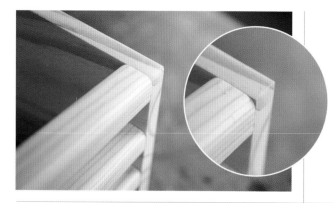

—26—

Sand uneven edges. A bit of sanding with some 150- to 220-grit sandpaper can blend uneven corners and edges for a much more finished look.

—27—

FIRE! Use a propane torch to darken the wood. Quick, smooth motion ensures even color distribution. For a rustic, worn look, torch everything a little extra then wire brush in the direction of the grain to make it stand out. Stain is an alternate option if you're not comfortable using a torch.

—28—

Install the brass screws. For extra points, align the slots so they all face the same direction.

—29—

Glue on felt pads. Use a little wood glue and some spring clamps to glue on the upper felt pads. Rounding or clipping the corners will really make these shine.

—30—

Add some bling. After the glue has dried, drill pilot holes and add brass screws to the corners of the felt.

BIKE RACK

Hang your ride high.

If you love making things using your hands, you probably also like going places using your feet. This slim wall rack for storing your favorite bike is a great way to marry those two passions. It's designed with a shoebox apartment in mind, and folds flat when not in use to reduce the chance of putting your eye out, kid.

DIFFICULTY

Easy

TOOLS & MATERIALS

- Tablesaw with crosscut sled
- Speed square
- Drill press with 1" Forstner bit, ¼" bit, ½" bit, and countersink bit
- Jigsaw
- Spindle sander
- Combination square
- Clamps
- Random-orbit sander
- Water-based stain
- Screwdriver
- Clear spray lacquer
- Sandpaper
- Mallet

BEHIND THE DESIGN

The rack is made from sturdy and slim ¾" plywood to keep things nice and flat when folded away. All of the hardware and rack features are hidden behind the cosmetic front pieces, which also function as the bicycle support arms.

ANATOMY

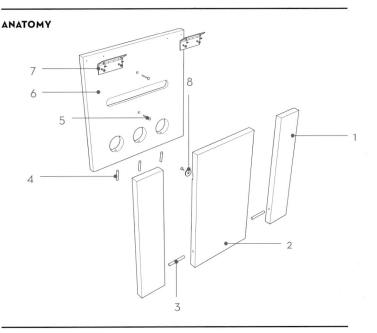

PARTS LIST

No.	Description	Qty	Details
1	Narrow support arm/face plate	2	¾" x 3" x 14"
2	Wide support arm/face plate	1	¾" x 3" x 14"
3	Metal rod	2	¼" x 3"
4	Hangers	3	¼" x 3"
5	Wood screws	2	#8, ½" long
6	Wall plate	1	¾" x 14" x 14"
7	Hinges	2	Cut to 2¹³/₁₆"
8	Fender washer	1	¾" diameter

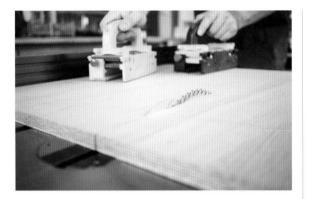

— 1 —

Prepare the stock. Rip the stock to width at the tablesaw using the dimensions listed on the previous page.

— 2 —

Crosscut the parts. Use a crosscut sled to cut the parts down to length, as listed on page 139.

— 3 —

Lay it out. Use a speed square to draw the centerline of the cutout in the wall plate of the bike rack.

— 4 —

Prepare the drill press. Choose a 1"
Forstner bit in order to accommodate the
¾" material thickness of the support arms.
It's also large enough to create a hole big
enough to accept the blade on your jigsaw.

— 5 —

Drill access holes. To prevent tear-out,
slowly lower the bit into the wood and drill
all the way through the stock.

— 6 —

Remove the waste. Mark out parallel
lines tangent to the access holes drilled in
each end of the rear plate. Use a jigsaw to
remove this section.

— 7 —

Sand it smooth. A spindle sander makes quick work of smoothing the interior edges of the cutout.

— 8 —

Lay out the hanger holes. Use a combination square to mark out a line 2½" from the bottom edge of the wall plate.

— 9 —

Drill it out. Use a 1" Forstner bit to drill three equally spaced holes along your layout line.

—10—

Make way for dowels. Centered on each of the hanger holes, use a ¼" bit to drill in from the end of the stock.

—11—

Create mounting holes. Above and below the cutout on the wall plate, drill and countersink holes to be used when screwing the bike rack to the wall.

—12—

Bore it out. On each face plate, drill ½" diameter holes about 2" deep into the inner edge of the narrower face, 3" up from the bottom end.

—13—

Clamp it up. Drill a hole about 2" deep on both sides of the larger face board, matching the 3" distance from the bottom. Insert one of the axles, and press the parts together with a clamp.

—14—

Make room for the washer. Use a Forstner bit that matches the fender washer you have to drill a shallow hole on the back side of the face boards, about 2" down from the top edge. Drill the hole so it overlaps onto the smaller face board about ⅛".

—15—

Secure it in place. Screw in the washer so it fits snugly into the hole. This will prevent the middle board from flipping outward when the rack is folded.

—16—

Smooth it out. Sand all of the parts to 220-grit using a random-orbit sander or by hand.

—17—

Apply a stain. To add color, use a rag to wipe on a waterbased stain.

—18—

Attach the arms. To connect the arms of the bike rack to the rear plate, install a hinge on each one.

—19—

Add a clear coat. Spray lacquer seals the stain and adds a protective finish coat.

—20—

Prepare the hangers. To create the hangers—for helmets, gloves, etc.—that are installed through the end of the wall plate and into the hanger holes, use ¼" dowels and chamfer the ends using sandpaper.

—21—

Set them in place. Tap the dowels into place on through the end of the wall plate. Leaving the hangers unstained adds a little visual interest to the design.

— How It Works —

What's better than a bike rack to hang your beloved bicycle? No bike rack! When you're off wheeling about town, this rack can collapse into a simple block of hanging wall art. Lovely grain, anyone?

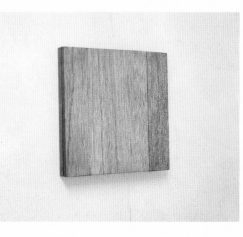

— Imperial To Metric Conversion —

Inches	mm*	Inches	mm*	Inches	mm*
1/32	0.79	17/32	13.49	2	50.8
3/64	1.19	35/64	13.89	3	76.2
1/16	1.59	9/16	14.29	4	101.6
5/64	1.98	37/64	14.68	5	127.0
3/32	2.38	19/32	15.08	6	152.4
7/64	2.78	39/64	15.48	7	177.8
1/8	3.18	5/8	15.88	8	203.2
9/64	3.57	41/64	16.27	9	228.6
5/32	3.97	21/32	16.67	10	254.0
11/64	4.37	43/64	17.07	11	279.4
3/16	4.76	11/16	17.46	12	304.8
13/64	5.16	45/64	17.86	13	330.2
7/32	5.56	23/32	18.26	14	355.6
15/64	5.95	47/64	18.65	15	381.0
1/4	6/35	3/4	19.05	16	406.4
17/64	6.75	49/64	19.45	17	431.8
9/32	7.14	25/32	19.84	18	457.2
19/64	7.54	51/64	20.24	19	482.6
5/16	7/94	13/16	20.64	20	508.0
21/64	8.33	53/64	21.03	21	533.4
11/32	8.73	27/32	21.43	22	558.8
23/64	9.13	55/64	21.83	23	584.2
3/8	9.53	7/8	22.23	24	609.6
25/64	9.92	57/64	22.64	25	635.0
13/32	10.32	29/32	23.02	26	660.4
27/64	10.72	59/64	23.42	27	685.8
7/16	11.11	15/16	23.81	28	711.2
29/64	11.51	61/64	24.21	29	736.6
31/64	11.91	31/32	24.61	30	762.0
1/2	12.70	63/64	25.00	31	787.4
33/64	13.10	1 inch	25.40	32	812.8

*Rounded to nearest 0.01 mm

ABOUT THE AUTHOR

Mike is a DIY enthusiast, author, and avid cyclist with a habit of taking things apart and putting them back together as he sees fit. He grew up in Georgia shootin' guns and tippin' cows, but now lives a much safer life as a sign maker in the San Francisco Bay Area.

INDEX

Note: *Italics* indicate a project

A

About the Author, 149

B

bamboo skewers, cutting, 28

Beer Caddy, 126

Beer Tap, 118

Bike Rack, 138

Box-O-Boo, 22

C

casters, installing, 87

centerpoints, marking, 34

Chip Off the Old Block, 62

circles, cutting, 34

circles, sanding, 35

cork, 67

countersinking, 20, 55, 58, 101, 112, 113, 135, 143

Critter Cavern, 104

cyanoacrylate, using, 27, 56, 135

D

dado blade, 65

dado, making, 15, 25, 65

E

Entryway Organizer, 12

exterior curves, sanding, 74

F

feet, making, 34

felt, gluing, 132

ferrule, installing, 124

flame finish, applying, 136

flushcutting, 92

frame, making a, 42

G

gluing up, 27, 36, 43, 72, 75, 79, 85, 98, 120, 134, 144

H

hole saw, 34

holes, drilling out, 73, 28, 141

I

Imperial to metric conversion, 148

K

knife storage, 22

L

lamp socket, assembling, 57

lamp, 48

Laptop Levitator, 76

laptop stand, 76

ledger strips, mounting, 27

M

Magnetic Frame, 38

magnets, installing, 19

magnets, making, 47

metal, smoothing, 44

mineral oil, applying, 29

miter gauge, using, 14, 15, 24, 32, 41, 51, 78, 86

P

peel-and-stick veneer, 44

pet bed, 104

pilot holes, drilling, 56, 88, 89, 110, 112, 113, 132, 137

Plywood Plinker, 96

pull chain hole, 57

R

rabbet, making, 16, 33, 40, 109

ripping stock, 24, 64, 78, 128, 140

router table, using, 18, 52, 74, 99, 109, 130

S

sanding a bevel, 53

sheet metal, 44, 115

sheet metal, curving, 116

slingshot band, attaching, 103

slingshot, 96

spindle sander, using, 73, 99, 108, 129, 142

spray adhesive, applying, 43, 44

spray finish, applying, 21, 37, 47, 75, 102, 125, 146

stain, applying, 145

Standing Desk Add-On, 93

Standing Desk, 82

Storage Blocks, 30

stretcher joint, making, 89-90

T

tablet stand, 62

templates, applying, 72, 79, 98, 107, 129

The Don Lamp, 48

The Headphone Hook, 68

thickness planer, using, 86, 128

thin boards, cutting, 70

tongue, making, 33

transferring hole locations, 112, 131

turnbuckles, installing, 91

turning, 122

U

UL knot, tying, 59

V

veneer, applying, 45

W

wax finish, applying, 117

wire hanger, making a, 46

Z

zero-clearance insert, 70

— PROJECT INDEX BY DIFFICULTY —

Easy

Beer Tap, 118

Bike Rack, 138

Box-O-Boo, 22

Chip Off the Old Block, 62

Entryway Organizer, 12

Laptop Levitator, 76

Magnetic Frame, 38

Plywood Plinker, 96

Storage Blocks, 30

The Headphone Hook, 68

Moderate

Beer Caddy, 126

Critter Cavern, 104

The Don Lamp, 48

Advanced

Standing Desk, 82

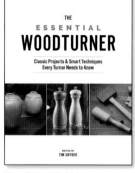

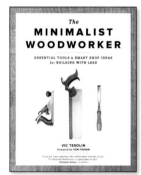
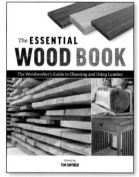
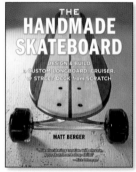
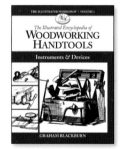
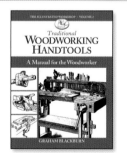
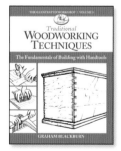